Shareholder-Driven Corporate Governance

Shareholder-Driven Corporate Governance

ANITA INDIRA ANAND

OXFORD
UNIVERSITY PRESS

OXFORD
UNIVERSITY PRESS

Oxford University Press is a department of the University of Oxford. It furthers the University's objective of excellence in research, scholarship, and education by publishing worldwide. Oxford is a registered trademark of Oxford University Press in the UK and certain other countries.

Published in the United States of America by Oxford University Press
198 Madison Avenue, New York, NY 10016, United States of America.

Library of Congress Cataloging-in-Publication Data

Names: Anand, Anita, 1967– author.
Title: Shareholder-driven corporate governance / Anita Anand.
Description: New York : Oxford University Press, 2020. |Includes bibliographical references and index.
Identifiers: LCCN 2019024888 | ISBN 9780190096533 (hardback) | ISBN 9780190096540 (pdf) | ISBN 9780190096557 (epub)
Subjects: LCSH: Corporate governance—Law and legislation. | Stockholders—Legal status, laws, etc.
Classification: LCC K1327 .A95 2020 | DDC 346/.06642—dc23
LC record available at https://lccn.loc.gov/2019024888

1 3 5 7 9 8 6 4 2

Printed by Integrated Books International, United States of America

Note to Readers

This publication is designed to provide accurate and authoritative information in regard to the subject matter covered. It is based upon sources believed to be accurate and reliable and is intended to be current as of the time it was written. It is sold with the understanding that the publisher is not engaged in rendering legal, accounting, or other professional services. If legal advice or other expert assistance is required, the services of a competent professional person should be sought. Also, to confirm that the information has not been affected or changed by recent developments, traditional legal research techniques should be used, including checking primary sources where appropriate.

(Based on the Declaration of Principles jointly adopted by a Committee of the American Bar Association and a Committee of Publishers and Associations.)

To my mother and father, Dr. Saroj D. Ram and Dr. S. V. Anand,
whose unwavering love and encouragement have inspired me
to fulfill life's promise.

Contents

Preface

Argument, Themes, and Purpose

This book examines prevailing conceptions of the corporation in light of developments in corporate governance since the introduction of the US Sarbanes-Oxley Act in 2002 and the global financial crisis (GFC) of 2008. In particular, its purpose is to explore the perplexing question of the extent to which corporations are beholden to the will of their shareholders. Thus, this book takes into account the practical realities that public corporations face, including increasingly complex legal regimes, shareholder activists, and volatile capital markets.

In recent years, shareholders have asserted more and more control over public corporations, no longer content to play the part of the passive owner. Perhaps in response to this pressure, legislators and regulators have grappled with the question of what protections shareholders should be afforded, particularly in the decade since the GFC. This shift in attitude by investors and regulators alike invites scholars to revisit the nature of the relationship between shareholder and corporation and to ask what role the law should play in affirming shareholders' ability to influence corporate governance.

The book introduces a new concept, "*shareholder-driven corporate governance*", or *SCG*. This term refers to an approach to understanding the corporation that seeks to protect shareholders' interests while also affirming their involvement in governance. It refers to both actual and potential governance strategies. *SCG* is a normative term in the sense that it presents a goal toward which lawmakers (not to mention investors) may aspire. It is also a descriptive term, explaining the ongoing phenomenon of a shifting balance of power that increasingly accommodates shareholder participation in corporate decision-making.

In exploring both positive and normative questions, this book examines the rise of shareholder activism across multiple jurisdictions, including the United States, the United Kingdom, and Canada. In these jurisdictions, members of boards of directors have fiduciary duties, but the following questions arise: How should boards discharge these duties in an age of shareholder activism? Does SCG change historical and current analyses of boards' fiduciary duties? Should SCG impact law-reform efforts? These broad questions lead to a consideration of three themes, which illustrate the importance of SCG and which are at the heart of this reexamination.

The first theme is the relationship between ownership and control in today's public corporation. My thinking on this topic is largely a response to Berle and Means's foundational argument that the modern corporation is characterized by the separation of ownership and control.[1] Modern capital market composition differs significantly from the Berle and Means model; today's shareholders are sophisticated, often seeking governance changes over and above those that yield a mere return on their investment. This reality, in turn, influences SCG initiatives: in some cases, public corporations with shareholders who demand greater accountability and more input, have been willing to respond and accede to shareholder demands by, for example, allowing shareholders to play an active role in nominating directors. It is not always the case that corporations accede to shareholder demands, of course. But the relationship among stakeholders has shifted in large part because of the increased sophistication of shareholders in the capital markets.

The second theme is a reevaluation of prevailing views of corporate law based on the phenomenon of SCG, and in particular increased shareholder activism. This analysis starts with the ideas contained in *The Economic Structure of Corporate Law*.[2] In that seminal book, Easterbrook and Fischel argue that the corporation is a nexus of contractual relationships (following Jensen and Meckling)[3] and that corporate law is "enabling." The law of contracts is often said to be enabling because it creates structures within which parties can make private arrangements, rather than requiring that anyone do anything in particular. Easterbrook and Fischel want to generalize this approach; rather than seeing corporate law as imposing a specific structure on organizations, they argue that it consists of default rules that apply in the absence of specifications contained in the contracts entered into by a corporation. These default rules serve as "off-the-rack" terms that fit a broad range of cases but can be tailored by the parties should their situation call for an altered fit.

While I agree that, broadly speaking, the nexus-of-contracts idea accurately describes the corporation and that corporate law is made up of default terms, I will contend that Easterbrook and Fischel's argument warrants reevaluation because public corporations are increasingly responsive to (or at least aware of) shareholder concerns, especially the concerns of institutional shareholders and blockholders. Shareholder activism has placed pressure on the default terms of corporate law in light of a shift toward greater involvement by shareholders in the functioning of the corporation. What form does this pressure take, and to what extent, if at all, should corporate law's default terms be amended? What does SCG mean for our thinking about corporate law? These new questions call for a reexamination of the nexus of contract model, which this book attempts to pursue.

Central to this book's conception of corporate law is the fact that public corporations are bound by prevailing legal regimes, including securities regulation, which is founded on investor protection and the admittedly nebulous idea of the "public interest." The enabling features of corporate law thus constitute only a subset of obligations to which public corporations must adhere; it is wholly inaccurate to examine enabling corporate law in the absence of other legal obligations. How should our thinking about securities law adapt to the emergence of SCG?

The book's third theme is the relationship between corporate law and securities regulation. Scholars too often overlook or misunderstand this relationship in their analyses of the public corporation generally and SCG specifically. Easterbrook and Fischel themselves barely consider securities law in their foundational framework. Yet as a practical matter, and to varying degrees depending on the country under consideration, these two areas of law have developed in separate legal silos and without relevant stakeholders being involved in the reform process. In addition, while both areas have been the subject of law reform, there has been little attempt to consider or reform these laws in concert. It is necessary to consider the relationship between these two areas of the law and the additional legal obligations, including disclosure rules, to which corporations are subjected once they become public, in order to understand SCG from a practical standpoint.

Thus, the importance of this book extends beyond a theoretical examination of the corporation. It has a normative undertone that could serve to inform policy formulation as well. If lawmakers are to pass legislation that responds to capital market developments, it is essential that they begin to understand SCG. With every rule proposed, they must first weigh its costs to market participants against its benefits to the public, which includes investors as well as issuers, financial advisers, and other market participants.[4] Despite its shortcomings, such a basic cost-benefit analysis must be premised on an understanding of the SCG phenomenon as conceptualized here.

This book serves as a resource on corporate governance both inside and outside of the academic environment. It will be relevant to lawyers, regulators, students, and scholars of corporate law, governance, and securities regulation. Many of these individuals may agree that the prevailing conception of the corporation as a hub of contractual relationships is somewhat outdated, and this book offers a more contemporary approach to corporate governance.

Context

While corporate-law scholarship exploded in the post-Enron period,[5] our collective thinking about the theoretical underpinnings of the corporation did not develop at a similar pace. The academic literature generally falls into one of three categories: the shareholder-versus-director primacy debate;[6] stakeholder theory including corporate social responsibility;[7] and law and economics scholarship or a critique of it.[8] Virtually all of this literature takes as its starting point the Berle and Means model of the corporation, with its foundational premise of the separation of ownership and control.

This book differs from the bulk of academic writing on corporate governance in that it does not adhere to the Berle and Means model of the corporation. Further, it does not fall neatly into any one of the three categories of corporate-law scholarship named above but instead draws on all three in order to grasp the implications of SCG. In bringing these three areas into conversation with one another, the book aims to complement the existing literature, which has increasingly focused on empirical examples of what I refer to as SCG. But what impact should developments in real-world capital markets have on our thinking about the corporation? For example, what does increased shareholder activism mean for theoretical conceptions of the corporation?

To my knowledge, no comprehensive study of governance has examined the theoretical implications of the SCG phenomenon in the context of existing thinking about the corporation. Perhaps the most important unanswered question is to what extent the concept of SCG is consistent with the idea that corporate law is "enabling." This book will rely on empirical studies to the extent that this is necessary to emphasize theoretical analysis and claims. To some extent, it will examine the corporation's incentives to adopt SCG reforms. For example, some firms may seek to stall SCG by implementing corporate governance mechanisms ex ante. They may also seek access to capital and therefore appeal to investors who may equate value with a comprehensive governance structure.[9] Finally, they may adopt SCG in order to discourage investors from concluding that a firm has a weak governance structure and thus a lower value.

This book seeks to make an original contribution to the literature on theories of the corporation through its formal exploration of a topic, which I call SCG, that is percolating in the literature but awaits comprehensive analysis. The book is a direct response not only to the emergence of activist shareholders but also to the claim that the model of the corporation in which shareholder primacy will prevail in major jurisdictions will become the standard legal model of the corporation.[10] The book is not specifically about shareholder primacy and shareholder value maximization, ideas that are central to debates about the scope of director fiduciary duties.[11] Rather, it examines the governance of corporations in light of both corporate law and securities law, positing the existence of a new way of thinking about the corporation altogether. Whether the issue is executive compensation, majority voting, or dual-class share structures, SCG requires us to focus on the importance of the shareholders' voice in the decision-making of the corporation.

Chapter Outline

Chapter 1 introduces the concept of SCG and sets forth the basic framework within which we may analyze capital market activity. This discussion begins from the possibility that while the shareholders who are said to "own" a corporation seek to maximize the value of their shares, the managers who control it may shirk their duties or divert corporate resources to their own benefit at the expense of shareholders.[12]

Responding to the potential for such conflicts of interest between manager and shareholder, as well as the very real possibility of management entrenchment, shareholders themselves may decide to monitor the actions of directors and managers, especially if they are institutional investors with significant financial resources. This desire to monitor is a cornerstone of SCG, and it directly opposes the idea that shareholders are merely passive investors. What else does SCG imply? After setting forth the framework for analyzing shareholders' role in today's corporation, the first chapter will outline the distinctive features of SCG (e.g., majority voting and proxy access). It will also point out differences in governance regimes across a number of countries and the impact of these differences on shareholders' interests.

Chapter 2 examines the existing conceptions of the public corporation and questions whether any of these ideas appropriately account for the rise of SCG. In particular, it examines the contractarian model of the corporation and considers the gaps in this theory (and its implicit call for private ordering rather than regulatory intervention) from the standpoint of SCG. This chapter also examines agency theory, which explains the division of ownership and control as an agency relationship that necessarily produces agency costs.[13] This idea is foundational for SCG because it provides the framework for understanding the problems to which SCG responds.

Chapter 2 also considers a newer and contrasting idea called principal cost theory, which argues that principal (or shareholder) control also comes at a cost, resulting from shareholders' lack of expertise and the potential for conflicts of interest among them.[14] This theory offers an important counterpoint to the normative arguments for SCG because it emphasizes the potential failings of shareholders and challenges the supposition that they are necessarily well positioned to play an active role in governance.

No one particular theory accounts for the rise of institutional investors and pension funds as monitors and activists or provides a complete answer to the normative proposition of SCG as an aspiration. Chapter 2 therefore engages with each of the theories outlined above in order to understand how and why SCG operates within the corporation and to illuminate the dangers inherent in SCG. It then considers the role of regulators in shareholders' relationships with the corporation, in light of the claim that this relationship is contractual.

Chapter 3 analyzes SCG through the twin concepts of shareholder democracy (the ability of shareholders to influence corporate affairs through voting and other mechanisms) and shareholder activism (the practice of shareholders asserting control over the corporation through the machinery of shareholder democracy). Taken together, these concepts are the vehicle through which SCG takes effect in practice.

The recent rise of shareholder activism conflicts with Berle and Means's thesis that shareholders lack control in the corporation. An activist shareholder who owns a sizable percentage of a corporation's equity can mitigate agency costs through two mechanisms that discipline management, namely, voice (direct intervention in the firm, as through control of voting rights or letters to management) and exit (the sale of shares, the threat of which imposes ex ante discipline on the managers).[15] These two avenues for activism put pressure on management to consider shareholders' perspectives, and the chapter analyzes how this pressure affects governance. Building on the theoretical discussion in chapter 2, chapter 3 considers how shareholder democracy limits agency costs and how lawmakers may balance this with the potential of increased principal costs.

Chapter 4 explores activism carried out by wolf packs. Just as a blockholder with a sizable percentage of the corporation's equity can significantly influence a firm's governance, a wolf pack is a group of investors that attacks a target corporation in tandem under the leadership of a single, sophisticated activist, collectively acquiring enough equity to form a de facto block. The chapter discusses the formation of wolf packs and conflicting theories that attempt to explain their behavior. It also focuses on their ability to acquire considerable power in a corporation. What does wolf pack behavior mean for SCG and the corporation? How should the law respond? These are the questions that chapter 4 aims to answer.

Chapter 5 examines multiple-voting share (MVS) governance structures. These structures put corporate control in the hands of a small group of shareholders who hold a minority of equity in the firm through special shares with many times the voting power of regular shares. As a result, this group of insiders is able to decide any given vote, while the rights of those who hold subordinate shares become largely meaningless. The corporation and its insiders thus manage to reap the benefits of public capital without accepting the burden of shared control, creating the potential for conflicts of interest between superior and subordinate shareholders. This chapter proposes a number of policy reforms aimed at empowering shareholders in firms with MVS, namely, mandatory sunset clauses, disclosure of shareholder voting, and buyout protections.

Chapter 6 examines change-of-control transactions and the use of the defensive tactic known as the poison pill, a governance tool that often puts boards, rather than shareholders, in charge of a corporation's response to a takeover. Much as we see in the MVS context, this separation of ownership of the corporation from its control may invite conflicts of interest, here between boards and shareholders. The chapter asks how SCG can and should inform regulation of this defensive tactic. It considers management entrenchment theory and the shareholder-primacy norm in the context of changes of control. Both the normative and the positive aspects of SCG make it necessary to revisit the current legal balance between the interests of directors and the interests of target shareholders in takeovers. The chapter considers the question of whether recent reforms to takeover-bid law reflect SCG.

Chapter 7 ties together the themes of the previous chapters in accordance with the central concept of SCG. It argues that the nexus-of-contract model continues to bear importance in analyses of the corporation but that this model only explains part of the story. While the corporation is certainly a hub of contractual relationships, it remains subject to the increasingly important phenomenon of SCG. The chapter examines policy choices in a regime that allows and facilitates SCG. For example, should law be two-tiered in the sense that it accounts for the relative sophistication of certain shareholders (e.g., institutions) compared with others (e.g., retail investors)? The chapter employs a cross-country approach, examining legal regimes in major common-law jurisdictions.

All in all, this book sets forth a new conception of the corporation which takes into account the ongoing shift toward greater shareholder involvement in corporate affairs. Some will argue that it is not new to say that shareholders have more power in today's corporation than they had in years past. The point of this book is not simply to make this basic claim. Rather, it is to reexamine the reality of shareholder activism and to ask how changing circumstances affect the balance of power between boards of directors and shareholders under securities and corporate law.

I would like to thank numerous people who have been influential in my thinking about the corporation and in assisting to bring this book to fruition. My research assistants, particularly Christopher Puskas, Davina Shivratan, Thoby King, William Maidment, and Richard Kennedy, have provided invaluable research and excellent editing, for which I am very grateful. Thanks also to Gail Henderson for her helpful comments on the manuscript and to Claire Hill for inviting me to present it at the University of Minnesota Law School. Over the past years, my colleagues Edward Iacobucci, Andrew Green, Arthur Ripstein, and Naizam Kanji have been extremely generous with their time in speaking with me about my research; I am always so grateful to hear their insights. My mentor, Michael Trebilcock, has encouraged me to push myself not only with respect to this book but also with regard to my scholarship in general. The impact that such long-standing and unfailing support has on a scholar's development is truly astounding, and I will always be grateful to him. My dear friend the Honorable Hal Jackman has been incredibly supportive of my academic endeavors. His influence on the development of my professional life, as well as my thinking about shareholders' interests, will always be present in my mind. And from the bottom of my heart, thank you also to my family—John, Anand, Sonia, Monica, and Kashia—whose love and support I cherish above all else.

List of Abbreviations

BJR	the business-judgment rule, a procedural rule requiring courts in the United States and Canada to take a deferential approach when reviewing business decisions by boards of directors.
CBCA	Canadian Business Corporations Act, the central statute governing corporate law in Canada.
CDPQ	Caisse de Dépôt et Placement du Québec, one of Canada's Big Eight pension funds.
CPP	Canada Pension Plan, one of Canada's Big Eight pension funds.
CSA	Canadian Securities Administrators, an umbrella organization for all of Canada's provincial and territorial securities regulators, through which these regulators work to coordinate and harmonize their efforts.
DCS	dual-class shares, a corporate structure under which some shares carry significantly greater voting power than ordinary shares, thus allowing a small group of insiders to control governance.
DGCL	Delaware General Corporation Law, the statute governing corporate law in the state of Delaware, which is the most important corporate regime in the United States due to the large volume of incorporations in that state.
FCA	Financial Conduct Authority, the conduct regulator for UK financial markets.
GFC	global financial crisis of 2008.
MVS	multiple-voting shares, those shares under a DCS or similar system that carry multiple votes per share.
OMERS	Ontario Municipal Employees Retirement System, one of Canada's Big Eight pension funds.
OSC	Ontario Securities Commission, Ontario's securities regulator.
OTPP	Ontario Teachers' Pension Plan, one of Canada's Big Eight pension funds.

SCG shareholder-driven corporate governance, a descriptive and prescriptive concept coined in this book, referring generally to an approach to corporate governance in which shareholders have significant influence.

SDS shareholder democracy scale, a graphic representation of the range of shareholder empowerment among different jurisdictions, allowing us to compare these jurisdictions according to the extent of decision-making authority they grant to shareholders.

SEC Securities and Exchange Commission, securities regulator for the United States.

USA unanimous shareholders' agreement, an agreement among all shareholders in a Canadian corporation limiting the powers of management and the board.

1

What Is Shareholder-Driven Corporate Governance?

1.1. Ownership and Control in the Corporation

According to Berle and Means's seminal treatise *The Modern Corporation and Private Property*, the rise of the public corporation fundamentally altered our notions of enterprise and private property by dividing ownership and control.[1] Classical economic theory assumed that the quest for profits would spur the owners of industrial property to use their property in the most efficient, profit-maximizing way.[2] Public corporations challenged this assumption by creating conditions in which the interests of the owners of property (i.e., shareholders) did not necessarily align with the interests of those in control of the corporation's assets.[3] In particular, corporations' economic power increased,[4] while shareholders became passive and apathetic with regard to the day-to-day administration of the business.[5]

Berle and Means argued that such shareholders were not behaving irrationally. On the contrary, it was cost-effective for them to be inactive in their relationship with the corporation.[6] In order to make an informed vote, shareholders would have to engage in time-consuming research, find and consider appropriate advice, consult with others, and weigh the alternatives. The costs of engagement simply outweighed its benefits. It made sense to allow managers to command the corporation and its assets with little shareholder resistance.

Shareholder-Driven Corporate Governance. Anita Indira Anand, Oxford University Press (2020).

DOI: 10.1093/oso/9780190096533.001.0001

Berle and Means's work dominated the corporate-law literature for decades.[7] However, the shareholder composition of the capital markets has changed a great deal in the years since they formulated their conception of the corporation. In the 1950s, individual investors held around 90 percent of the US equity markets, while institutional investors held only 6 percent. Today institutional investors hold around 66 percent of the equity market.[8] Many of today's shareholders cannot be classified as rationally apathetic retail shareholders; rather, they are sophisticated, often seeking governance changes in addition to a return on their investment. Some are hedge funds that look for undervalued companies that they can purchase and turn around.[9] Others are institutional long-term investors, such as pension funds, seeking stable investments on behalf of beneficiaries to whom they owe a fiduciary duty. These types of investors differ significantly, but one commonality is clear: these are not the shareholders to whom Berle and Means referred in their writing.

Gilson and Gordon argue that the rise of shareholder activism has led to a reconcentration of ownership in the hands of institutional investment intermediaries. They assert that this change has occurred because of the privatization of retirement savings (and the corresponding funding required) and capital market developments that favor investment intermediaries offering low-cost diversified investment vehicles.[10] Yet this "reconcentration" does not capture the full gamut of activist pressure. Activists may engage in two basic types of activism: offensive activism, primarily initiated by hedge funds targeting a poorly performing company to take over and reform; and defensive activism (the type Gilson and Gordon describe), involving institutional blockholders who take on an advocacy role when they are unhappy with the corporation in which they are invested.[11]

The Industrial Revolution elevated the factory to the dominant form of production, separating the worker from control over the instruments of production.[12] When large public corporations entered the market, the owners were also separated from the means of control over production.[13] Today a similar historic shift is taking place, as we seem to be experiencing a reunification of ownership and control. This new era has emerged because institutional shareholders have largely replaced retail investors as the predominant shareholders in the public corporation. The era of corporate governance dominated by the retail investor is over. Today's shareholders, including activists and institutional shareholders, are anything but passive. They are often minority shareholders who uncover or respond to concerns of agency costs and view shareholder participation as necessary because of the "marked tendency for management to perpetuate itself in office."[14]

The rise of sophisticated shareholders over the past twenty-five years, namely, hedge funds and pension funds, undermines the contemporary relevance of Berle and Means's argument that the modern corporation is characterized by the separation of ownership and control, and particularly their observation that "the position of ownership has changed from that of an active to that of a passive agent."[15]

Given these dramatic changes in the composition of capital markets, scholars have offered analytical concepts to explain corporate governance today.[16] Bainbridge, for example, argues that we have shifted away from the era of the Berle and Means manager-controlled corporations and entered an age of "new corporate governance" where boards of directors retain the ultimate right of fiat.[17] As a result of activism, best-practice guidelines, changes to director compensation packages, market pressures, and various legal reforms including stock-exchange and securities-law reforms mandating more director independence,[18] boards have transformed from passive rubber stampers to active, controlling agents of the firm. Bainbridge calls this "director primacy," a phenomenon defined by two tenets: the corporation organized and run as a hierarchy with the board of directors on top; and this board of directors guided by the goal of maximizing shareholder wealth.[19]

Here we can pause to identify, in factual terms, the means and ends of corporate governance. Few will argue with the idea that there is a tension between shareholder and director interests as described above. However, a crucial starting point for an analysis of this tension is that the law attributes broad power to boards on the basis that directors are agents of the corporation who, legally speaking, must act with a view to the best interests of the corporation, which include but are not limited to shareholder interests. Corporate law is premised on the idea that this duty of loyalty to the corporation is a means to further shareholder or stakeholder interests, not the interests of directors themselves. In fact, courts give deference to board decision-making under the business judgment rule (BJR), which presumes that directors reached their decisions in good faith with an honest belief that they were acting in the best interests of the corporation.[20]

Bainbridge builds on and defends this deferential approach. While he acknowledges that imperial CEOs are undesirable,[21] he views the historic separation of shareholders' ownership and board control not as a problem to be solved but as a unique invention that has allowed modern corporations to flourish. Accordingly, he argues that efforts to give shareholders more power should be resisted, as shareholders suffer from inferior information and divergent interests, making them poor decision makers (at least in terms of the entire organization).[22] Every large organization needs a model that facilitates effective decision-making. Placing the ultimate decision-making authority on the board of directors, Bainbridge argues, strikes the appropriate balance between authority and accountability.[23] Consequently, shareholder voting only exists as an "accountability mechanism of last resort," such as in the event that managers and directors have performed well below expectations and are therefore subject to a takeover fight worth waging.[24]

While Bainbridge persuasively argues that shareholders may make poor managers given their lack of information and divergent interests, I will argue that corporate law should not view shareholder participation in governance as a tool of last resort. The sophistication of institutional shareholders and activists is a defining difference between the shareholders of whom Berle and Means (and Bainbridge) speak and the shareholders to whom SCG draws our attention. In light of this sophistication and the meaningful input that shareholders can provide, it makes sense to allow shareholders greater scope for participation in the affairs of the corporation. Of course, corporate law already allows shareholders to communicate with one another and, if they disagree with the decisions of the board, to participate in governance via the dissident-proxy process. It also allows them to file shareholder proposals and to requisition shareholder meetings. These rights are part of a broader statutory framework that, along with securities regulation, is designed to protect investors generally and circumscribe the power of the board.[25]

Shareholders, especially of the institutional variety, are increasingly sophisticated corporate monitors. It is therefore legitimate that they should seek greater participation in a corporation's governance, including meaningful access to the nomination processes for electing directors (so-called proxy access) and majority voting.[26] Thus, as I argue in this book, we have entered a new phase of corporate governance where shareholders, particularly hedge funds and other institutional shareholders, are more emboldened and more influential in corporate governance.

What does this argument mean for theories of corporate governance? To what extent should corporate law, and our theoretical understanding of corporate law, change to account for the growth of shareholder activism? What, if anything, should be the regulatory response? These are the questions this book explores. To help navigate these questions, the book is based on a concept I call shareholder-driven corporate governance, or SCG. As suggested above, SCG is a broad-based analytical concept that refers to the trend in corporate governance whereby shareholders participate in the governance reforms that public corporations adopt. *Participation* is defined broadly: it does not merely refer to increases in shareholders' direct voting power; rather, it encompasses reforms that reduce opportunities for managerial entrenchment (boards and management alike) and that generally increase the ability of shareholders to become involved in the day-to-day operation of the business.

1.2. The Emergence of SCG

SCG is both a normative and descriptive term. It is normative in the sense that it is aspirational: it is a goal toward which law reformers or corporate-law scholars have reason to aim. Perhaps those who agree with SCG as an objective to be achieved will have differing viewpoints on how, in fact, it should be reached or what reforms should be implemented in order to further SCG. Perhaps they will differ regarding what are the end goals of SCG. But the conversation about SCG as an aspiration occurs in a conceptual space that is normative.

SCG is also descriptive in the sense that it refers to the current shift in the balance of power in public corporations today. In jurisdictions throughout the world, reform agendas and board decision-making evidence a movement toward what I am referring to as SCG. Companies are choosing reforms to voluntarily appease, or at least respond to, shareholders. For example, anyone who watched the collapse of Enron and WorldCom, resulting in vast investor loss, and the subsequent press coverage and debates in the US Congress at the turn of the century may reasonably have expected increased government action and tighter regulation. Firms began to examine their own governance mechanisms in light of the potential implementation of more stringent requirements.[27] As the *American Journal of Strategic Finance* stated in 2007:

> Recent reports suggest that private companies are already adopting SOX initiatives voluntarily. According to some analysts, hard economic times have played a part in private companies' newfound interest in corporate governance. Taking steps toward acting like a public company, or becoming "SOX ready," could lower the risk for acquisition-minded companies and their underwriters, placing the target in a competitive advantage. Other benefits might include reductions in lending and insurance costs.[28]

Even large Canadian companies (including Canadian National, Magna International, and TD Bank) began to adopt SOX-like[29] reforms, such as voluntary certification of financial statements.[30] As noted in previous work,[31] these companies were cross-listed and would ultimately bear a domestic legal responsibility to certify their financial statements. But at the time they began to certify their financial statements, the legal requirement had not yet come into force,[32] and foreign issuers wondered whether they would be required to comply with SOX at all.[33] In short, these activities suggest that corporations are sensitive to shareholder demands, or at least the potential for shareholders to be demanding. Of course, the extent of their sensitivity will depend on the laws of the jurisdiction. Unlike the United States, many developed countries—especially in Europe—have long had in place strong shareholder protections as well as shareholder-centric corporate law.[34] Corporations' increasing responsiveness to shareholder-friendly reforms is apparent in the general response to the aftermath of the Dodd-Frank[35] legislation and the implementation of more robust clawback provisions in the United States.[36] For more than a decade, executive compensation has been a major governance issue. One the one hand, compensation schemes can provide managers with efficient incentives to maximize shareholder value.[37] On the other, these schemes can be emanations of rent-seeking and agency problems. A proposed SEC rule within Dodd-Frank would require companies to clawback compensation to executives in certain events and prohibit companies without such clawback provisions written into their contracts from listing. At the time of writing, eight years after the initial proposal, the SEC's chairman maintained that this provision will eventually become law, although the delay has raised doubts.[38]

Despite no proposals for mandatory clawback provisions to curb executive compensation in Canada, 60 percent of firms on the S&P/TSX 60 now have clawback provisions, compared with merely 22 percent in 2011. Of the thirteen companies that are neither dual-listed nor OSFI-regulated, seven have clawback provisions, as compared with three in 2011.[39] This suggests that clawback policies have become more common for large companies despite an absence of mandatory regulation. Such trends are likely due to a combination of the Dodd-Frank legislation in the United States and the inclusion of clawback provisions in the best-practices guidelines of the OSFI in Canada.[40] This is an example of SCG "in action": over and above existing law, public companies seem to be more responsive to shareholder concerns.

This discussion of executive compensation suggests that there are differences between traditional corporate governance and shareholder-driven corporate governance that warrant further study. Table 1.1 isolates five metrics on which we can evaluate the conceptual differences between the two approaches to corporate governance. From this table, it seems clear that traditional characteristics of corporate governance have been altered somewhat by the introduction of potential reforms that can be grouped under the rubric of SCG.

1.3. Explaining the Change

If it is true that SCG is on the rise, it is natural to seek an explanation for this phenomenon. Why are we increasingly witnessing

Table 1.1 Differences between two types of governance.

	Traditional corporate governance	Shareholder-driven corporate governance
Director fiduciary duties	Yes	Yes
Shareholders' ability to nominate directors	No	Yes
Majority voting	No	Yes
Prohibition on dual-class share structures	No	Yes
Executive compensation/ mandatory clawback provisions	No	Yes

SCG "in action"? Public companies recognize the importance of major shareholders for their ability to raise capital and benefit the company's reputation. Adopting SCG reforms may be a means by which to deter investors from devaluing the firm. If management does not implement governance changes that are requested or desired by shareholders or if management withholds information related to its governance practices, investors may be more likely to conclude that the firm has something to hide or that the information being withheld is bad news.[41] The expected cost of such investor discounting on the firm's value is so high that firms believe they are better off implementing governance changes and engaging in proactive disclosure.[42]

Voluntary reduction in managerial power due to market pressures can be seen in the shift in board structure from a managerial model to a monitoring model, where outside shareholders exercise some influence on corporate decision-making. A further explanation for this change is that the capital markets began to perceive monitoring models as economically superior to alternative arrangements. As Eisenberg notes in his review of what appears to be a collective paradigm shift, if not a vicious cycle over time, social norms play a large role in the belief systems of actors in the corporate community, and the tenets by which these actors abide by change over time. For board structures, best-practice guidelines strongly endorsed monitoring boards, which eventually spurred the investment community to believe that there was an economic advantage to monitoring boards. Investors subsequently put pressure on firms to adopt monitoring boards with more independent directors, perhaps because of the public shaming that would ensue if they did not. Boards that did not adopt the structure became subject to criticism in public forums such as *Businessweek*'s list of twenty-five worst boards or the Annual List of Underperforming Companies.[43] Thus, social norms became catalysts that eventually spurred the creation of monitoring boards as a means to avoid criticism and pressure from the capital markets.[44]

In short, social norms and investor pressure play a significant role in encouraging firms to adopt SCG voluntarily. In an environment of increasing investor advocacy,[45] ethical investing,[46] and skepticism of corporate motives,[47] robust disclosures rank high at the top of investors' priorities list, especially in the case of sophisticated investors[48] such as pension funds.[49] As Hoffmann explains, if corporate managers fail to comply, they risk being challenged:

> When activists are discontented with management's adaptation to shareholder demands, they do not hesitate to challenge the executives' authority. In many cases, they push for and achieve adjustments in corporate governance structures and processes. Shareholder activists do not shy away from directly attacking senior managers and even pursuing their resignation if they do not comply with shareholder demands.[50]

It will come as little surprise, therefore, that firms are likely to respond to and adopt SCG for self-interested reasons.[51] They have their reputations and credibility to protect.

Contrary to Berle and Means, we are witnessing a move toward the unity of ownership and control. This shift is not occurring solely in North America; internationally, corporations are engaging in SCG and voluntarily adopting governance practices that enhance shareholders' rights. But the point of this book is not merely to recognize a phenomenon, that is, the rise of shareholder activism and the increasing unity between control and shareholding, but also to ask what our legal response should be. Whether regulators are attuned to the incentives for SCG is unclear; we may never know why regulators propose and implement particular pieces of regulation. On the one hand, they may seek to enhance investor protection or maintain market efficiency. On the other hand, they may seek to maintain a close relationship with capital market participants, including boards of directors and senior management, if they plan on returning to the private sector after finishing their terms as regulators.[52] In other words, securities regulators may have self-serving motives that rest outside of their statutory obligations, and they may indeed pursue and implement particular regulation with these alternative motives in mind.[53]

Regulatory incentives are not the central issue in this book; we do not need to know with certainty why regulators do what they do. It is enough to accept that SCG among corporations exists and has the potential to grow. The questions then become: What are the implications of SCG on how we conceptualize the corporation? From a practical perspective, how does SCG alter our approaches, and indeed theories, pertaining to the role of (and the need for) regulation? It is to these questions that we turn next.

2
SCG and Corporate Law Theory

2.1. Introduction

Building on Berle and Means, scholars have traditionally considered publicly traded corporations to be characterized by a division between ownership and control: a group of largely passive shareholders own shares in the firm, while control is held by expert managers who are specially situated to make decisions. In recent decades, and particularly since the GFC, this state of affairs has begun to change as activist shareholders have taken (or been given) greater control of the corporation.

The fact that management and the board have been at the helm of corporate governance has led to the assumption, at least in some quarters, that this is their rightful place. This idea that management and the board, rather than shareholders, are best suited to steer corporate governance is supported by the contractarian model of the corporation, which suggests that the interest that investors have in public corporations is entirely defined by the bargain they have made with the issuers. When investors buy shares, they rationally accept some risk in order to make some gain. The most commonly identified contract, or, more accurately, quasi-contract, consists of the articles of incorporation and corporate by-laws, otherwise known as the firm's constating documents. The articles include the characteristics of the shares that investors purchase. These documents are quasi-contracts because they set out the terms according to which the corporation functions, and shareholders invest on the basis of these terms. This contractarian model suggests that corporate law operates in the background of the transaction

Shareholder-Driven Corporate Governance. Anita Indira Anand, Oxford University Press (2020).

DOI: 10.1093/oso/9780190096533.001.0001

between investor and issuer, serving to uphold the parties' bargain; the law is merely a system of default terms that apply in the absence of any explicit contract between or among corporate stakeholders.

One weakness in the contractarian model as a basis for corporate governance is the fact that, unlike in many contractual settings, there is little or no negotiation between the contracting parties when shares are purchased. In addition, the corporation may have in place a unanimous shareholders' agreement, or USA. In a USA, common in closely held firms, shareholders divide their responsibilities and set out the rules relating to exit conditions, such as the procedures for when a shareholder wishes to sell his or her interest in the firm. In the absence of a USA, the firm's articles and by-laws represent the agreement—the terms of the legal relationship—between the corporation and the shareholders. This means of establishing terms is very different from a debt relationship, in which the debt holder has the specific terms of the contract explicitly stated in a debenture or other debt agreement with the corporation.

Furthermore, in modern securities transactions, there is usually an intermediary who receives a commission upon executing a trade on behalf of investors. These commissions may be known to the investor, or they may be embedded in the purchase price. Regardless, there is little negotiation and agreement between the shareholders and the corporation, especially when one thinks about trading in the secondary market, where securities frequently change hands with little reference to corporate disclosure relating to the securities in question. As this chapter argues, the contractarian approach fails to account for the complexities in modern financial markets.

It is no doubt possible to analyze corporate law through the contractual paradigm, but it does not follow that shareholders' rights should be entirely a matter of private agreement. Shareholders may be insufficiently protected by the bargains they make with issuers, especially in change-of-control transactions. Securities law is at least partially premised on this very point, given its goal of protecting investors even after they become shareholders (or security holders) in a corporation. The principles of SCG demand that we look beyond the contract and revisit established theories of corporate governance in order to better understand the "bargain" in which investors find themselves. SCG highlights the fact that regulators, rather than merely setting default contractual terms, have an important statutory role to play in protecting investors through the imposition and enforcement of mandatory regulations.

The next two sections set forth established thinking about the corporation. Section 2.2 examines the contractarian model for the corporation. Section 2.3 analyzes some of the recognized factors that inform the formation of shareholder contracts, namely, agency costs and principal costs. The rest of the chapter reconceptualizes the corporation in the context of SCG. Section 2.4 considers shareholders' interests and asks what role regulation plays in protecting these interests over and above contractual and quasi-contractual relationships. Section 2.5 examines the mandate of securities regulators in relation to the interests of shareholders. Section 2.6 concludes.

2.2. The Contractarian Model of Corporate Law

The contractual approach at the heart of discussions of corporate law stems from Coase's article "The Nature of the Firm," which lays out an interpretation of the corporation based on contractual relationships. The firm, he argues, is a substitute for a series of contracts.[1] It reduces costs because owners do not have to make continuous contracts with the individuals who are crucial to running the business.[2] For example, rather than continually contracting with individuals to sew garments, a clothing company can hire these individuals as employees within the firm. Coase asserts that the firm is effectively made up of a multiplicity of these types of internal contractual relationships.

Building on Coase's work, Jensen and Meckling introduced the concept of a "nexus of contracts,"[3] interpreting the firm as a hub or locus of contractual relationships for individuals within and outside the firm. In their view, all of the corporation's relationships can be understood as contractual, whether the contracts are with suppliers, trade creditors, banks, shareholders, debtholders, and so on. Jensen and Meckling explain that this "nexus for contracting relationships . . . is also characterized by the existence of residual claims on the assets and cash flows of the organization, which can generally be sold without permission of the other contracting individuals."[4]

In a series of articles, Easterbrook and Fischel set forth what has become the dominant framework for analyzing the corporation.[5] They characterize the corporation as being "a complex set of explicit and implicit contracts." In their view, corporate law "enables the participants to select the optimal arrangement for the many sets of risks and opportunities" that arise in capital markets.[6] Because no one set of terms will be best for all parties, the law should not be unduly restrictive. Apart from an antifraud rule, managers and directors should not be restricted in their attempts to act in the corporation's best interests.

Underlying this approach is the premise that corporate law is a wholly private enterprise, despite corporations' enormous scale and extensive social impact.[7] Rather than setting out to protect the public in any generalized way, corporate law should simply amount to a standard-form contract that supplies the terms that parties would have agreed to if they had entered into a formal contractual arrangement.

Easterbook and Fischel argue that in most instances, corporate law provides such terms, functioning as the background contract containing the terms that parties would have negotiated "were the costs of negotiating at arm's length for every contingency sufficiently low."[8] In their view, corporate law serves to make transactions more efficient, because parties do not have to spend time negotiating terms to which they would likely otherwise agree.[9] According to Black, corporate law's default terms are trivial, because corporations effectively structure their governance as they please and may not need to rely on these default terms at all.[10] Later in this chapter, I will dispute this "triviality hypothesis."

Of course, these scholars acknowledge that mandatory corporate-law rules exist. For example, directors on corporate boards must operate within the bounds of antifraud laws. They are also required to comply with their duty to act in the best interests of the corporation.[11] However, contractarian scholars argue that such mandatory terms cover situations that either matter very little or would be adopted by parties if they thought about them. When firms do not adopt an efficient governance structure, markets will encourage the removal of these suboptimal structures over time. Thus, the best actors to determine contractual and legal efficacy are capital market participants themselves, and there is no need for (extensive) mandatory corporate-law provisions.[12]

According to the contractarians, corporate law's main purpose is to minimize transaction costs by reducing the costs of drafting, negotiating, and continually updating terms.[13] These scholars see corporate law as a pragmatic, instrumental tool serving simply to mark out a commercially expedient arrangement into which individuals would choose to enter in private transactions.[14] Corporate law should thus mimic bargaining outcomes that actors would have achieved privately had they turned their minds to them.[15]

There are four tenets underlying this approach to corporate law: (1) a view of corporate-managerial power as normatively unproblematic; (2) a general belief that investors are collectively, if not individually, capable of making rational and efficient normative decisions; (3) a strong preference for micro-level private ordering over macro-level state intervention; and (4) a belief that market-based organization is superior to other regimes.[16]

Another way in which scholars describe corporate law is as a "gap filler." In other words, when the terms of the contract or quasi-contract are silent, the statute will fill in the gaps with substitute or "default" terms. This is helpful not only for parties in a contractual relationship (so that they know what their rights are) but also for courts that may need to understand the legal relationship and, ultimately, attribute liability on the basis of this relationship. As Easterbrook and Fischel state, "the gap-filling rule will call on courts to duplicate the terms the parties would have selected, in their joint interest, if they had contracted explicitly."[17] Corporate law is useful because it serves as "a set of terms available off-the-rack so that participants in corporate ventures can save the cost of contracting."[18]

This gap-filling role is useful because a corporate charter is necessarily incomplete. Corporations are made with an eye to the future, and governance structures are designed to regulate over long periods of time.[19] Specifically, gaps often emerge in charters for two reasons: the transaction costs make it too costly to specify an arrangement for each issue, or a novel contingency that the initial charter failed to address arises.[20] For example, the development of the market for hostile takeovers in the 1970s and 1980s required public officials to create new default rules to govern problems that emerged in this new business environment. Companies that went public in the 1970s simply did not predict the development of the poison pill or the ways boards could interact with poison pills to deter hostile takeover.[21]

As these scholars point out, corporate law's default terms can generally be amended by the parties, for example, by amendments to the constating documents or via a unanimous shareholder agreement. Therefore, the default terms are, in a sense, voluntary. In the absence of explicit negotiation (as might be found in a unanimous shareholders' agreement), the terms include rules that mandate the following: that equity shares have one vote per share, that these votes can be used to elect directors, and that debt investors do not have participatory rights in the governance of the firm.[22]

Easterbrook and Fischel focus primarily on US corporate law: what states' corporate statutes say in the absence of contractual arrangements between managers and shareholders. They explain how, with fifty states offering differing rules of corporate law, managers can choose the geographical place to incorporate that is most desirable to investors. The managers who choose the location of incorporation in such a manner will steer the corporations to jurisdictions that attract the most money.[23] But these managers may not select the jurisdictions in which shareholders' interests are best protected. According to the "race to the bottom" line of reasoning, states compete in granting corporate charters and adopt statutes that are more lenient on corporate managers in order to garner more incorporations.[24]

Easterbrook and Fischel's theoretical exposition of the function of corporate law is foundational. Broadly speaking, the nexus-of-contracts model on which this exposition is based offers an accurate description of the corporation. Of course, the relationships within the corporation are contractual. However, this does not mean that the contract captures every aspect of these relationships. Easterbrook and Fischel do not provide a comprehensive account of "the corporate contract," because they do not comprehensively consider the firm's obligations under other areas of law, particularly securities regulation.[25] I will consider the ways in which securities regulation complicates the contractarian model later in this chapter.

Not all scholars agree with the approach put forward by Easterbrook and Fischel. For instance, Blair and Stout developed an opposing view, which they call a "team production theory" of corporate law.[26] They contend that corporations "can be understood as solutions to team production problems, rather than as property."[27] To underscore the difference between the team production and the contractual theory of corporate law, Blair and Stout assert, "In reality, the public corporation is not so much a 'nexus of contracts' (explicit or implicit) as a 'nexus of firm-specific investments,' in which several different groups contribute unique and essential resources to the corporate enterprise, and who each find it difficult to protect their contribution through explicit contracts."[28] Boards of directors play a valuable role in mediating among several groups, a role that the nexus-of-contracts account of the firm cannot explain.

The debate over the nature of the corporation has another dimension: what is the purpose of the board of directors? In order to begin to answer this question, it is necessary to look closely at the relationship between shareholders and directors/managers as principals and agents.

2.3. Agency Theory and Principal Cost Theory

In addition to developing the idea of a nexus of contracts, one of Jensen and Meckling's key contributions relates to the rationale underpinning corporate law generally. They described the relationship between managers and owners as one of agency[29] and argued that when firms contract, the ultimate goal is the reduction of agency costs.[30]

An agency relationship is one in which one or more persons (principals) engage someone to perform some service on their behalf (the agent). In order to help the agent accomplish this end, the principals necessarily delegate some authority to the agent. If both parties are utility maximizers, the agent may not always act in the best interests of the principal, and it is generally impossible for the principal to monitor the agent at zero cost. The resulting agency costs occur in three forms: (a) monitoring costs borne by the principal to ensure that the agents are fulfilling their responsibilities; (b) bonding costs expended by the agents to provide assurance that they are doing their jobs responsibly; and (c) the overall residual loss, which is the dollar equivalent of the reduction in welfare expenditures by the principal due to agent divergence.[31]

In corporate law, managers act as agents for the shareholder principals. The assumption is that there is a separation between ownership (shareholders) and control (management), potentially enabling management to act in self-serving ways. Thus, in accordance with the contractarian model of the corporation, when securities are sold to outside shareholders, the purchasers assume that the managers are maximizing their own welfare and therefore bid down the price of the securities. To increase the securities' selling price, managers offer monitoring devices in the form of corporate-governance features, such as independent directors, accountants, and a promise not to engage in self-dealings. Competition is assumed to work to ensure that firms with the most effective modes of reducing agency costs gain a competitive advantage, so suboptimal contracts will die out over time.[32]

Agency theory has been hugely influential in explaining a wide range of corporate-governance relationships that exist between shareholders, boards of directors, and officers.[33] In particular, agency theory's description of the relationship between management and shareholders in the context of widely held corporations has been generally accepted. When there are a large number of small shareholders, individual shareholders tend to have neither the power nor the incentive to devote significant resources to monitoring and correcting the actions of management.[34] Thus, a shareholder contract (or a regulatory framework) that minimizes agency costs will be one that does not allow managers to stray from protecting the corporation's interests.

Agency theory informs the concept of SCG because it isolates the loss that shareholders can experience when directors or managers become entrenched. Agency costs inevitably appear wherever an elected group of representatives runs a public company, and this book argues that it is the role of law to minimize these costs. In the next chapter, I elaborate on the relationship between agency costs and shareholder democracy, which is the state of affairs that arises when shareholders take an active role in governance.

Recently, some scholars have criticized agency theory as incomplete. Goshen and Squire reject what they call "agency cost essentialism," the idea that corporate law and securities regulation serve chiefly to reduce agency costs. The authors propose a new concept called principal cost theory.[35] Shareholders, they argue, should be concerned not only with managers' interests conflicting with their own (imposing agent-conflict costs) but also with three other types of cost: principal-competence costs (arising from investor mistakes due to a lack of expertise), agent-competence costs (arising from honest mistakes by management), and principal-conflict costs (arising from conflicting interests between investors).

Principal cost theory heavily emphasizes the contractual element of corporate governance and offers a strong defense of private ordering. Goshen and Squire argue that the question of how to arrive at the optimal arrangement that will reduce costs overall is firm-specific. Every business arrangement involves a tradeoff among the four types of costs, and empirical studies find no consistent relationship between the degree of shareholder empowerment and overall financial performance. Therefore, they recommend that firms should be able to create their own optimal arrangements, with regulations operating only as default rules that can easily be changed by contracting parties.

Principal cost theory is important for SCG in its contextualism: it points to the potential for shareholders to make decisions that undermine corporate welfare, whether due to incompetence or conflicts of interest with other shareholders. Shareholders are generally not experienced managers, nor are they bound by a fiduciary duty to the corporation. Therefore, it is clear that any theory of the shareholder's role in the securities market must take into account the limits of shareholder-centered governance and the dangers that emerge when inexpert or conflicted shareholders have too much power over the corporation. Chapter 4 offers an in-depth exploration of a scenario with the potential to create considerable principal-conflict costs, namely, takeovers by "wolf pack" activists.

However, it is important to note that principal cost theory and its arguments for private ordering do not detract from the underlying normative argument for SCG, which is that investors have a legitimate interest in corporate governance worth protecting. As this book argues, shareholder activism is usually carried out, or led, by large institutional investors with the sophistication to mitigate principal-competence costs. Meanwhile, regulations should be in place to curb potential principal-conflict costs where they might arise, as we will see in the context of the wolf pack.

No single theoretical paradigm of the corporation suffices to explain the ongoing shift away from the traditional, management-centric model toward SCG. Each of the concepts discussed above has a role to play in our analysis of corporate governance. In reconceptualizing the corporation, therefore, we must consider the contractual and quasi-contractual relationships that make up the corporation. We must also be careful to take account of agency costs as well as principal-conflict and principal-competence costs. With all of this in mind, we now turn to the question of how corporate law theory can and should inform regulation.

2.4. Shareholder Concerns and the Role of Regulation

The central argument of this book is that shareholders, and therefore their interests, are fundamental to corporate governance and that corporate law theory warrants an adjustment to account for the increasing sophistication of shareholders, among other things. Accordingly, this book rejects the contention put forward by Black that corporate law is trivial.[36] It argues that this area of law, as well as securities regulation, has an important role to play in SCG's development. Unlike corporate law, the purpose of securities regulation is to ensure that investors are protected. Across jurisdictions, the regulatory mandate is unequivocal on this point.[37] While investors and the corporation can "agree" on the terms of the corporate contract, a regulatory agency will seek to ensure that investors are protected. This mandate means that, notwithstanding its contribution to our understanding of the corporation and indeed corporate law, contract law does not fully explain the corporation's legal obligations as a whole.

Empirical analysis also supports the claim that, contrary to Black's triviality hypothesis, corporate law has a significant impact on shareholders. Listokin argues that in the late 1980s, a wave of nonmandatory antitakeover statutes entered many corporate legal regimes. These statutes included "fair price," "business combination," and "control share acquisition" statutes which limited the ability of hostile acquirers to take control of public companies. Different states chose different statutory regimes. In states without fair-price statutes, only 20 percent of companies chose to write fair-price protections into their charters. Conversely, 56 percent of companies in states with a menu option for fair-price protection, and 98 percent of companies in states where fair-price protection was the default rule had fair-price protection.[38]

These results contradict the hypothesis that corporate law is trivial, which would predict that if a company desires a certain arrangement, it will simply write corporate contracts to get into or out of that arrangement. In other words, the triviality hypothesis assumes that companies will naturally attain the same desired level of corporate governance regardless of the different statutory regime chosen by a state, which Listokin's study clearly contradicts.[39]

Academia has not understood, or at least not understood well, the extent to which the securities regulatory mandate affects corporate governance. These two separate areas of law[40] have developed via different legislative processes and are subject to separate statutes and regulatory authorities. Historically, as outlined in *Santa*

Fe Industries, a common demarcation of corporate law and securities law has been an internal versus external distinction. Corporate law was said to govern the internal affairs of the corporation, while securities regulation would deal with external affairs, such as the overall relationship between investors and the capital markets in which they invest.[41]

However, such a neat distinction does not work in practice. When an amendment occurs in one realm, say, in the corporate-law sphere, it affects the many public corporations subject to securities regulation. Yet no coordination exists between the development of laws in these two areas, thus resulting in overlap and sometimes conflict. Specifically, there are three principal sources of conflict between corporate law and securities law. First, conflict can occur due to jurisdiction. Under corporate law, a firm is only subject to one statute based on where it chooses to incorporate, whereas a firm must comply with the securities law in all the jurisdictions in which it has significant investors.[42]

Second, there are significant differences in enforcement mechanisms. Corporate-law violations are generally brought to court by private parties, while securities regulation is administered through specialized regulatory bodies.[43] Third, each has different fundamental goals. A goal of corporate law is to compel corporations to ensure sound internal governance, so it primarily focuses on directors' and managers' responsibilities, duties, and liabilities on the one hand and shareholders' rights on the other. Securities law has a much wider scope of consideration, focusing on protecting investors and fostering of fair and efficient capital markets, both of which include shareholders, debtholders, and the public (made up of investors and potential investors) generally.[44]

One example of conflict can be found in the duties of directors in Canada. Corporate law imposes statutory duties on directors and officers, while securities regulators purport not to regulate in this sphere. They nevertheless impose rules that impact the duties owed by directors and controlling shareholders. Vanderpool and

Waitzer argue that the activity of securities regulators in this respect marginalizes corporate law's statutory duties of directors. Complaints are brought to regulators rather than courts, and are framed in terms of public interest and shareholder rights rather than directors' statutory duties. As a result, corporate law relating to directors' duties fails to develop, creating a doctrinal gap that securities regulation is not able to fill.[45]

Also affected are shareholders' rights. Indeed, these two parallel regimes conflict with each other; shareholders' rights contradict directors' authority in corporate law. For example, we see such conflict in the regulation of defensive takeover tactics: securities regulators have the power to override the business judgements of the board to allow shareholders to decide on a proposed sale of a company.[46] Some commentators argue that this may be inconsistent with the duties and authority granted to boards under corporate law.[47] This inconsistency creates uncertainty in the law, which is not advantageous for corporations or investors and inevitably produces costs for courts, regulators, and corporations themselves.

As I will argue, the public corporation is more than simply a nexus of contracts.[48] Rather, it is a body made up of contractual relationships, which are, in turn, subject to the legislative mandate of securities regulators. That mandate can override the intentions of the firm and its shareholders as expressed in their initial contract. While some may argue that this conception is no different from the nexus-of-contracts model, it should be noted that no amount of voluntary contracting can thwart the securities regulatory mandate which ensures (or at least seeks to ensure) that investors—of whom shareholders are a subset—are protected. This mandate is not a "term" in the contract. It is an additional regulatory layer that stands alongside, or perhaps above, the corporate contract or quasi-contract. Parties themselves may not know when the securities regulator will intervene in their transactions or other corporate conduct.[49]

The securities regulatory layer is mandatory, and it applies regardless of circumstances. Boards of directors, courts, and tribunals cannot pick and choose when securities law applies.[50] To state the obvious, securities regulation emanates from law passed via the democratic lawmaking process. The securities regulator has a mandate to fulfill, and this mandate is fundamental to understanding the constraints that affect the public corporation in modern times.

Admittedly, Easterbrook and Fischel consider securities regulation to an extent, but their argument is normative rather than positive. Opining on what securities regulation should be, they explain that "less is more" in terms of firm governance. They argue, "Markets that let particular episodes of wrongdoing slide by, or legal systems that use deterrence rather than regulatory supervision to handle the costs of management, are likely to be effective in making judgments about optimal governance structures."[51] Their rationale is that the costs of knowing about a firm's governance are low and that over time, the competitive process will shape the optimal structure of a firm's governance.[52] The implication is that optimal governance structures evolve over time; they cannot and should not be mandated.

This view is no doubt appealing to many who believe that unregulated capital markets do not undermine investor protection. They reason that investors are rational and can protect themselves by reading a firm's disclosure.[53] But behavioral finance has shown that this assumption is false. Investors, especially retail investors, are not always rational. They do not take into account all available information prior to making their investment decisions.[54] Rather, they may be driven by herding behavior, in which investors rush to sell or buy securities based on little or no evidence that would justify such behavior.[55] The mere plausibility of this thesis suggests that we cannot assume that investors will be adequately protected under a system with few regulatory safeguards. Furthermore, capital markets with these characteristics are unlikely to flourish.[56] Investors will not flock to markets in which it is uncertain whether they will receive protection, regardless of whether they would act rationally in a given instance.

Investors' capacity for irrational behavior is illustrated in a study of UK investor habits. Specifically, the study showed that investors did not evaluate the reasoned arguments for corporate noncompliance before deciding whether or not to accept it (by investing in the corporation). [57] Investing in a noncompliant corporation before evaluating the reasons for noncompliance is an irrational behaviour. To be clear, corporate noncompliance is acceptable because of corporate governance rules passed in the United Kingdom in 1992 deployed a comply-or-explain regime, a regime that both Canada and Australia have also implemented.[58] This regime allows corporations to be noncompliant with guidelines if they disclose an explanation for doing so.

These results suggest that investors, especially retail investors, do not take into account arguments for noncompliance. Instead, contrary to the assertion that investors are consistently rational and will protect themselves by reading a firm's disclosure, investors may use financial performance as a proxy to determine if noncompliance should be excused. One may argue that this means the flexibility of corporate governance is working as intended, since it allows firms to customize their structures as they see fit, with investors rewarding them accordingly. However, it also suggests that investors are driven primarily by immediate economic gain rather than long-term protections and thus may potentially ignore material information in making their investments. It is these risks that securities regulators are meant to manage for the well-being of not only investors but also capital markets as a whole.

Before examining the mandate of securities regulators, it is worth pausing to consider a contractarian reply to the argument presented above. SCG is premised upon shareholders' increasing awareness of the importance of a firm's governance structure and their place within it. Even if sophisticated shareholders wish to participate in a firm's governance, one might think that they would work such terms into their relationship with the corporation. In other words, if shareholders are so sophisticated in today's market, why can't they negotiate terms into their contractual and quasi-contractual dealings with firms?

To claim that shareholders are sophisticated is not to claim that their interests are automatically immunized from moral hazard or their own suboptimal deliberation. Contractarian logic of pareto-optimality trades on a conception of informed, rational decision-making that does not always align with the concrete circumstances to which securities regulation responds. It does not follow from the fact that bargaining *can* facilitate shareholder preferences that these arrangements will always be available without regulatory oversight and intervention.

What's more, not all investors are sophisticated. Retail investors may not appreciate the importance of bargaining for greater rights, or they may not care enough to do so.[59] As a result, appealing to contractual relations alone cannot offer retail investors needed protections. The obligatory nature of securities regulation ensures that irrationality and limited bargaining power are not barriers to shareholder protection. Retail and institutional shareholders, not to mention the integrity of the market itself, benefit from the protective framework offered by securities regulation, to which we now turn.

2.5. The Mandate of Securities Regulators

Why is it so important that we treat securities regulation as an added layer to the corporate contract? This theoretical consideration matters for two reasons. First, the way in which boards conceptualize their duties currently (and rightly) emanates from corporate law. That is, boards see themselves as having a duty to act in the best interests of the corporation. Neither this duty nor the body of law from which it flows should be understood in an

Austinian fashion. That is to say, the architecture of corporate law is more than a system of commands backed by sanctions. Corporate law facilitates, indeed encourages, voluntary relationships between corporations and shareholders by establishing a framework for this relationship, including directors' duty to act in the best interest of the firm. The state's regulatory apparatus, though, does have a role to play in this process. Boards of public companies must also recognize the potential "long arm" of the securities regulator. This long arm allows regulators to stop a transaction or to prosecute corporate executives for violating the public interest.

Second, the role of securities regulators matters for investors who are served when the securities regulator fulfills its mandate. It is not simply the corporate contract that defines shareholders' rights but also the actions and objectives of the securities regulator, which ostensibly provide greater protection. What precisely is the mandate of securities regulators? The mandate of the Securities and Exchange Commission (SEC) is "to protect investors, maintain fair, orderly, and efficient markets, and facilitate capital formation."[60] In the United Kingdom, the role of the Financial Conduct Authority (FCA) "includes protecting consumers, keeping the industry stable, and promoting healthy competition between financial service providers."[61] Similarly, the Ontario Securities Commission (OSC) has a mandate "to provide protection to investors from unfair, improper or fraudulent practices, to foster fair and efficient capital markets and confidence in capital markets, and to contribute to the stability of the financial system and the reduction of systemic risk."[62]

Despite the many differences among these jurisdictions, the far-reaching mandates of their securities regulators are strikingly similar. In each case, the regulator has been charged with maintaining the well-being of the market as a whole and with protecting the general investing public. This role differs considerably from the objective of corporate law, which is aimed at establishing norms for private relationships. The existence of these regulatory bodies makes it impossible to explain the corporation entirely in terms of contractual and quasi-contractual relationships. After all, these firms must operate under securities regimes in addition to abiding by a jurisdiction's corporate law.

Ontario case law demonstrates how the investor protections enacted by a securities regulator can have a significant impact on the way corporations operate in a given jurisdiction. Following the Supreme Court of Canada's decision in *Asbestos*,[63] the OSC's power to uphold the public interest must be considered as a means to preserve and protect the capital markets.[64] Thus, neither shareholder votes nor the actions taken by a firm in the name of fairness are sufficient to determine whether a transaction is in the public interest. Rather, case law dictates that the term *public interest* has a forward-looking element in which the interests of the capital markets must be taken into account more broadly.[65] Investors have undisputed interests in receiving accurate disclosure and investing in markets in which insider trading is not tolerated.

For example, in *Re Biovail Corp.*, the OSC held that it could rule that conduct was contrary to the public interest even in the absence of specific violations of the OSA. Specifically, when exercising its public-interest jurisdiction, the regulator will consider "all the relevant circumstances" pertaining to a case, which the court considered to include policy considerations and the interests of all parties that may be affected by the matter.[66] Similarly, in *Sterling Centrecorp Inc.*, the OSC affirmed that the commission's "public interest" jurisdiction is broad and powerful and that its duty extends to the capital markets as a whole.[67] In *Costello v. Ontario (Securities Commission)*, there was no technical violation of the securities act, yet the OSC held that Costello's conduct was contrary to the public interest. The OSC reaffirmed that its public-interest jurisdiction is preventive and prospective in nature and oriented toward the prevention of future harm to the capital markets.[68] The case of *Cornish v. Ontario (Securities Commission)* also highlighted that general deterrence is an appropriate consideration when deciding a case.[69]

Of course, securities regulators across jurisdictions will interpret their mandates differently. The distinct structural features of each commission, as well as its respective legislative mandate and the political regime in which it operates, produce distinct sets of securities rules.[70] However, across these jurisdictions, there remains the common thread of a regulatory body charged with enacting protections for the benefit of investors and the capital markets as a whole. These bodies are an essential component of the legal matrix in which a corporation exists, wherever it is incorporated. The existence of securities regulation must have a corresponding effect on our thinking about the public corporation itself.

Securities regulators complicate the story told by the contractarian school. Easterbrook and Fischel are aware of the issues posed by the mandatory nature of securities regulation for the contractual framework that they put forward, although they are skeptical of the benefits of securities regulation for investors.[71] In trying to justify securities regulation's mandatory rules, they argue that preventing fraud and providing information via mandatory disclosures are the primary and perhaps only justification for securities law. This argument seems misguided given corporate frauds during the global financial crisis (GFC) of 2008, in which investors lost millions of dollars as a result of their investments in the financial markets.[72]

The justifications for securities law are perhaps less important to an understanding of SCG than the explicit mandate of securities regulators. In order to reconceptualize corporate governance, this book focuses not on what would be the ideal mandate of securities regulators but on how, in practice, they execute their mandate as it actually exists in statute and case law and what this implies for public corporations. It suggests that corporate law and securities law cannot be fully understood separately, especially with regard to the public corporation. Thus, the corporate contract as conceived by Easterbrook and Fischel is only part of the story. The rest will be told in the chapters that follow.

2.6. Conclusion

Law plays a role above and beyond setting out default contracts for private parties. It is instrumental to protecting shareholders, especially retail shareholders, who may otherwise be vulnerable. It is true that the corporation, at its most basic, is a group of voluntary private relationships. However, the law posits a complicated balancing act required to protect shareholders' interests, assuming that investors cannot be left to fend for themselves as contracting parties. As discussed in chapter 1, history highlights the need for meaningful regulation, particularly the 2008 GFC and the accompanying investor losses. The next chapter considers how shareholders are able to protect their interests in the corporation (at least partially) when they have the power to do so.

3

Shareholder Democracy and Shareholder Activism

3.1. Introduction

One of the motivations underlying this exposition of SCG is the growth of shareholder activism, a phenomenon that has become an increasingly conspicuous aspect of capital market activity over the past twenty-five years. The term *activist investor* describes an institutional investor that seeks value-enhancing changes in the leadership, governance, capital structure, or strategy and operations of a corporation in which it is invested. There are two basic types of activism: offensive activism, in which a hedge fund takes over a poorly performing firm and then reforms it to enhance its performance; and defensive activism, in which the activist institution takes on an advocacy role when it is unhappy with a corporation of which it already holds a significant block.[1]

Who are the shareholder activists of the world? They are institutions, typically hedge funds and pension funds, that participate in corporate governance to varying degrees. Contrary to the conventional Berle and Means paradigm of the modern corporation in which ownership is separated from control, the rise of shareholder activism suggests that shareholders of these corporations have begun to reassert control over the companies in which they hold shares.[2] SCG views shareholder activism as a necessary means to curb management entrenchment.[3]

What does the law say about shareholder activism? To begin, the law actually permits shareholder participation in the governance of

Shareholder-Driven Corporate Governance. Anita Indira Anand, Oxford University Press (2020).

DOI: 10.1093/oso/9780190096533.001.0001

the firm. Securities and corporate law allow shareholder proposals and requisitions and compel corporations to provide shareholders with proxy forms and meeting circulars prior to every shareholder meeting. The law also permits shareholders to put forward motions by circulating a separate or "dissident" circular.[4] Activists argue that these corporate-law rules are insufficient; legal changes to prevent management entrenchment and ensure meaningful shareholder participation in the corporation are required.[5]

Shareholder democracy refers to the ability of shareholders to influence the corporation through their votes. It is an important concept in corporate law, one that underpins the legitimacy of shareholder activism. But shareholder democracy is not a static concept, nor is it universally adopted. Jurisdictions can experience more or less shareholder democracy depending on the substantive content of their respective corporate-law statutes. This chapter examines the relevant empirical literature and argues in favor of increased shareholder democracy, in the form of shareholder representation in director nominations, in order to make the existing right to elect directors meaningful. Shareholders' right to elect directors is pointless if shareholders themselves do not also have a say in choosing the candidates for whom they are voting.

Section 3.2 explores the concept of shareholder democracy as the main justification for recognizing the legitimacy of shareholder participation in the corporation. Section 3.3 analyzes the function that activist shareholders play in monitoring the corporation's management and board. It also responds to the main argument against increased shareholder democracy, namely, "short-termism" on the part of hedge funds. Section 3.4 examines the unique role that pension funds play in the capital marketplace. Section 3.5 considers the need for regulatory reforms that will realize increased shareholder democracy, focusing in particular on proxy access. Section 3.6 concludes.

3.2. Shareholder Democracy as the Basis for SCG

Berle and Means argued that the separation between ownership and control is a characteristic of many modern public corporations.[6] While shareholders may seek to maximize the value of their residual claim, managers may shirk their duties or divert corporate resources to their own benefit at the expense of shareholders.[7] According to Jensen and Meckling, these divergent interests can lead to agency costs, which arise when shareholders delegate decision-making authority to directors and officers, thereby establishing a potential fissure between the interests of agent and principal. This moral hazard prompts rational shareholders to expend resources monitoring the behavior of their agents and incentivizes directors and officers to incur "bonding" costs to guarantee that the shareholders' interests are fully pursued.[8]

Contrary to empirical evidence,[9] some argue that predictions regarding proliferating agency costs, which include managers overcompensating themselves, are overblown and that managers do not entrench themselves.[10] However, as long as it is *possible* for management to prioritize its own interests above those of the corporation and its stakeholders, then agency cost analysis remains relevant. Chapter 6 considers the effects of entrenchment in the context of takeover bids. This corporate activity offers a particularly clear picture of the costs that emerge when managers have both the incentive and the opportunity to prioritize their own jobs over the value of the firm.

Shareholder democracy has the potential to decrease agency costs. The greater the shareholder democracy, and the added accountability it provides, the less entrenchment there will be. Given the balance of power between the board of directors and shareholders in a jurisdiction, a "shareholder democracy scale" (SDS) looks as illustrated in figure 3.1.[11]

Figure 3.1 Shareholder democracy scale.

Consistent with SCG, some scholars believe that shareholders should have a strong voice in corporate governance in order to ensure that management and the board act in shareholders' interests. Bebchuk, for example, has advocated for reform that would empower shareholders to nominate directors on the corporate ballot, to vote by secret ballot, to initiate changes to corporate charters, to vote on compensation, and to remove directors.[12] At least some shareholders would benefit from these reforms in terms of the power they wield within the corporation, of course, but the reforms would also "induce value-enhancing changes without shareholders exercising their power to intervene."[13] Once relations between shareholders and management are framed by the former's power to intervene, the latter has reason to avoid the costly exercise of this power by pursuing shareholder value in the first place. The idea is that shareholders' capacity to intervene will often be enough to keep management's conduct in harmony with shareholder interests.

By contrast, those who favor director primacy argue for retention of power in boards and indeed more insulated boards, believing that shareholder democracy creates costs that could outweigh its purported benefits.[14] As Lipton and Savitt argue, proposals for shareholder empowerment would

> transfer the basic responsibility of corporate management from directors to shareholders. And . . . leave management and directors subservient to the whims of shareholders . . . no matter how inconsistent with long-term corporate performance, and no matter how destructive to the economy as a whole.[15]

Lipton and Savitt favor less shareholder involvement in corporations so that boards can serve corporations as they are legally required to do.[16] The sharp disagreement between Bebchuk's thesis and this view highlights the polarized debate. However, members of both camps probably recognize that corporations are more democratic in some jurisdictions than in others.

In practical terms, Canada's corporate-law regime sits somewhere in between the two poles (see figure 3.2) but likely closer to director primacy, because Canadian corporate law grants boards the power to act in the best interests of the corporation but does not favor director primacy to the exclusion of shareholders' influence altogether.[17] In particular, shareholders can make written proposals for consideration by management, requisition meetings if they hold a certain minimum percentage of votes, and bring actions for conduct that is oppressive or unfairly prejudicial to their interests.[18] Recently proposed amendments will mandate majority voting among other reforms designed to increase shareholder participation in corporations.[19]

We can argue, therefore, that Canada's legal regime supports shareholder democracy to some extent, allowing shareholders to have some influence in the governance of corporations. The important role of shareholders is most evident in recent reforms to takeover-bid law under which bids are subject to a

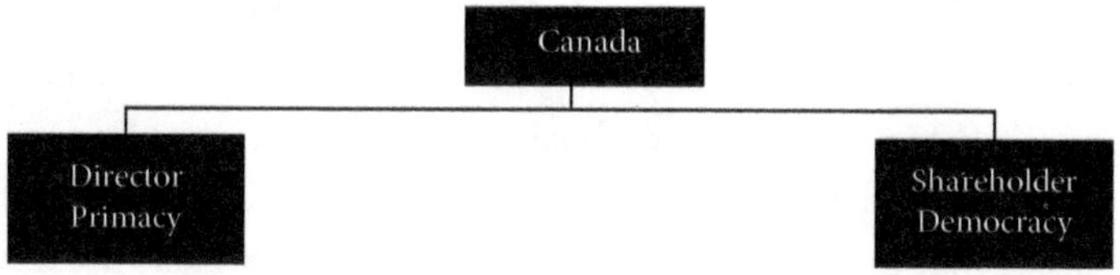

Figure 3.2 Canadian corporate law on the shareholder democracy scale.

mandatory (that is, unwaivable) minimum tender condition of more than 50 percent of all outstanding voting securities of targets, excluding those already held by the bidder and its joint actors. Bids can, therefore, only succeed with the support of a majority of independent shareholders. In essence, a bidder must obtain a majority of the shares held by others before it can take up shares.[20]

By contrast, law in the United States, particularly Delaware, affords more deference to the business judgment of directors, providing them with a great deal of flexibility to make unfettered decisions.[21] While Canadian boards are also protected by a business-judgment rule, it differs from the US iteration. In the United States, courts have set forth a strong but rebuttable presumption that board decisions are well informed, made in good faith, and in the interests of the corporation.[22] In order to rebut this presumption, a party must demonstrate gross negligence.[23] This rule has been seen as necessary to allow boards the freedom they supposedly require in order to make decisions without fear of liability for honest mistakes.[24] Delaware law gives robust statutory protection to directorial authority through DGCL § 141(a), which Sharfman describes as "provid[ing] the Board with almost unlimited authority to manage the corporation."[25]

Under Delaware law, if a court determines that a board of directors acted in good faith and in accordance with its fiduciary duties, the board is legally entitled to preserve the long-term strategic goals of the corporation. This is true even if a majority of shareholders favors an alternative approach.[26] In a takeover-bid situation, for example, US boards are entitled to "just say no" to a proposed bid and to use defensive tactics, such as poison pills, to prevent (as opposed to simply delay) a bid.[27] Once it becomes apparent that the target company will be sold or broken up, however, the board's duty shifts to maximizing shareholder value, either by negotiating for improved bid terms or by seeking out and proposing an alternative transaction.[28] US law thus falls closer to the director primacy side on the SDS (see figure 3.3).

The law regarding directorial duties in the United Kingdom tends to put considerably more emphasis on shareholder empowerment compared with Delaware. The deferential business-judgment rule, so central to American corporate law, is not recognized in the United Kingdom, nor is the standard for breach so high.[29] For most of the twentieth century, UK courts used a standard similar to Delaware's "gross negligence" rule for review.[30] Then a series of cases in the 1990s dispensed with this laissez-faire approach to directorial conduct and adopted a stricter, objective standard, now codified in the Companies Act 2006.[31]

Despite their divergence of views, both Bebchuk and Lipton would likely agree that the shareholder democracy debate is about the extent to which we wish to carve out directorial power in favor of increased shareholder decision-making. But they would disagree about where on the scale corporate law should situate itself. This question of the appropriate parameters of corporate law is at the heart of SCG. Recall that SCG does not simply describe the phenomenon of increased shareholder activism. It also forces us to ask how much power should shareholders should have.

This question is difficult to answer because of "overlap" among stakeholders. For example, directors and other decision-making insiders are often themselves shareholders. This narrow category of shareholders is able to exercise considerable influence

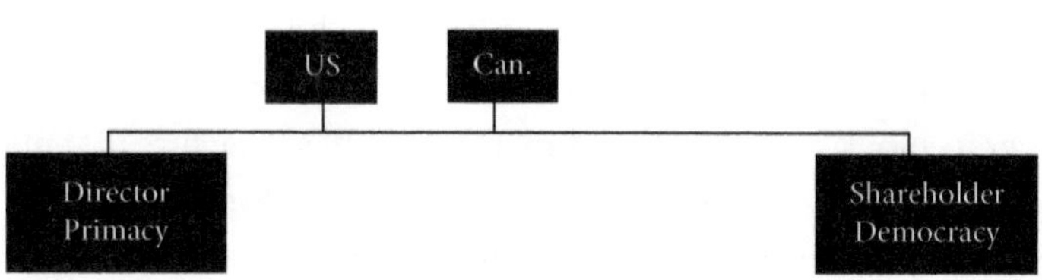

Figure 3.3 US and Canadian corporate law on the shareholder democracy scale.

over companies without relying on the mechanisms of shareholder democracy. Rather, the shareholders most affected by the democracy debate are those on the outside who have to become "activists" in order to make their voices heard. These "outside" shareholders have a distinct and important role to play in the public corporation. We now turn to an analysis of the potential benefits of activism.

3.3. Shareholder Activism and Monitoring

(a) Monitoring Role

The presence of an activist or institutional shareholder that owns a sizable percentage of a corporation's equity can mitigate agency costs through two mechanisms that discipline management, namely, "voice" and "exit".[32] Of these alternatives, voice involves the activist's direct intervention in the firm, often through letters to management, shareholder proposals, or the exercise of control or voting rights.[33] Accordingly, managers may act in the interests of shareholders (or at least those of the activist) out of fear of replacement. Exit involves the sale of the activist's shares. The sale can have the effect of driving down the firm's share price, thereby punishing management ex post.[34] The threat of exit imposes ex ante discipline on managers.

An activist's ability to monitor management and the board is essential to its decision to exercise either voice or exit. The larger the activist, the more readily it can absorb the costs of monitoring. The larger its block of shares, the more reason it has to ensure that management is held accountable, since it has more "skin in the game."[35] The activist intervenes when the private benefits of doing so outweigh the costs. Empirical evidence suggests that there is a positive, or at least a neutral, relationship between the presence of activists and firm value.[36] Activists are associated with improved outcomes for shareholders on matters ranging from executive compensation to the facilitation of takeover bids.[37] The benefits provided by the activist's monitoring flow to other shareholders, who are able to free-ride on the large shareholder's activism.

Of course, activists' incentives to monitor, including their willingness to internalize the costs of free-riding, vary with the size of their block.[38] Small investors can only absorb a negligible share of the firm's risk, leaving them with insufficient incentives to monitor.[39] Put another way, only large activists will monitor firms with high monitoring costs.[40] Evidence further suggests that multiple small activists are not as effective in influencing corporate decision-making as single large activists, partly because coordination costs between the small activists impede their ability to monitor the firm.[41] This means that a group of small shareholders that collectively owns a large block of shares will likely provide less effective monitoring than would a single large activist with a block equivalent in size and right.[42] It is simply more difficult to organize behavior among a group of dispersed shareholders,[43] especially when shareholders have heterogeneous preferences, as they often do.[44]

In short, the presence of a single activist can have a beneficial effect on the firm's governance in reducing agency costs through monitoring. Blocks made up of multiple small activists may be less effective at fulfilling the role of the activist in the corporation. While one might generally assume that activists are institutional shareholders, this is not to say that retail shareholders have no monitoring role to play. Retail investors could also be important in monitoring corporate management. We have seen retail pressure grow in the area of environmental and social governance (referred to as "ESG"), where grassroots lobby groups and shareholder proposals have made an impact on corporate agendas during the proxy process.[45]

(b) Short-Termism

While activists play an important monitoring role in public corporations, they are subject to the standard accusation of "short-termism." This refers to the possibility that activists are concerned only with short-term gains to be made by the corporation and may therefore make decisions that do not provide ongoing long-term benefits to the company as a whole.[46] This criticism is premised on the belief that the activists' supposed short-term objectives are likely to conflict with the long-term best interests of the corporation and its other shareholders.[47] However, it is important to note that looking out for the short term is not necessarily inconsistent with doing the same in the long term, especially when inefficient leadership is at the helm of the corporation.

The foremost goal of an activist, and particularly a hedge-fund activist, is to maximize investors' returns.[48] As unregulated entities, hedge funds search for and invest in high-yield products and projects on behalf of clients who have entrusted their money to the fund.[49] While hedge funds may focus on the short term to maximize their immediate returns, the focus may well coincide with the long-term interests of corporations.

The 2011 change of control at Canadian Pacific Railway (CP) demonstrates the potential for alignment between activist shareholder interests and long-term value creation at target firms. In 2008, CP's performance began to lag behind other major North American railways. For example, by the end of 2008, CP's operating ratio sat at 80 percent, while the operating ratio of Canadian National Rail (CN) was only 66 percent. In 2011, hedge fund Pershing Square Capital Management formally announced that it had acquired 12 percent of CP's shares. CP appointed two new board members and offered a board position to Bill Ackman, founder and CEO of the activist shareholder Pershing Square.

Ackman rejected the offer, and Pershing initiated a proxy battle, eventually proposing a slate of seven new directors.

During the battle, the sitting CP board continued to support then-CEO Fred Green, whereas Pershing Square proposed Hunter Harrison, former CEO of CN. Citing the company's poor performance, CP's major shareholders publicly declared support for Pershing's director slate. Six CP board members, including Green, declined to stand for reelection. The Pershing slate was elected to the board, and Harrison was appointed CEO.[50]

Contrary to the claims of many naysayers, Pershing's actions served the long-term interests of CP. Even after Pershing divested about one-third of its 24 million shares (which represented a 14.2 percent stake in CP) in October 2013, CP stock closed at CAD$147.95 a share, which was more than triple the value when Pershing first began purchasing CP shares. Jang reported:

> Harrison has led a turnaround at CP, narrowing the efficiency gap between it and rival CN. Analysts have been surprised at the pace of CP's improvements, including achieving faster average train speeds and reducing the time that locomotives are parked in rail yards.[51]

At the time, CP's third-quarter profit was CAD$324 million, the best quarterly results in the corporation's history.[52]

The CP example reveals that shareholder activism can be positive for corporations even in the long term. But such activism has not been uniformly beneficial for corporations. Proxy contest data have yielded mixed results.[53] A 2010 victory by Lionsgate management over shareholder activists was followed by a share price increase of more than 100 percent over the next two years,[54] while a similar victory by EnerCare management also saw share price significantly increase over the next two years.[55] However, a victory by the management of Baja Mining Corporation over shareholders was followed by a 99 percent decrease in share price.[56] Meanwhile, a victory by shareholder activists over the management of Hudbay Minerals was followed by a subsequent share price decrease, in contrast to the example of CP above.[57] These examples are consistent with the argument of Rose and Sharfman that while shareholder activism can provide value, its benefits should be evaluated on a case-by-case basis.[58]

Shareholder activism may not be uniformly beneficial for corporations, but when it does yield benefits, they accrue to all shareholders, not only to the activist or hedge fund. Becht et al. find that the average abnormal return at target firms in the forty days surrounding the disclosure of activist intentions is 7.0 percent in North America, 4.8 percent in Europe, 6.4 percent in Asia, and 6.4 percent globally.[59] This North American result is nearly identical to what Brav et al. found in the United States during the period from 2001 to 2006. Their study found an average between 7 and 8 percent abnormal return in share price during the forty-day period straddling the announcement of an activist campaign.[60] Similarly, Carrothers points out in a 2013 study that the average buy-and-hold abnormal return in the twenty months after the disclosure is 23 percent.[61] This result was not offset by a subsequent long-term decrease in stock price.[62] In short, it appears that the market as a whole can benefit from positive responses to hedge-fund activism.[63]

Consistent with the position described above, Katelouzou argues that the dark side of hedge-fund activism is largely a myth: "activist hedge funds are not short-term investors . . . [the] evidence makes a case for hedge fund activism as a value-enhancing corporate governance mechanism which could plausibly be corporate governance relevant."[64] Target share price movement following a proxy contest suggests that shareholder activism, including the ability to assert a position that differs from management via dissident nominees, can be beneficial for firms.

3.4. Pension Funds as Institutional Investors

Canadian pension funds have a distinct and important role as some of the most significant players in Canadian and global financial markets. Their investment capacity is broad, their influence is significant, and their diverse asset classes offer enviable returns while mitigating risk. These funds have invested more than CAD $600 billion across different asset classes, broken down into roughly two-thirds debt and public or private equity and one-third alternative asset classes such as real estate and infrastructure.[65]

These huge institutional investors collectively hold approximately 15 percent of the total assets of Canada's financial system. The eight largest public pension funds (the Big Eight) control two-thirds of this 15 percent, with more than CAD$1 trillion net assets under management. These funds include Canada Pension Plan (CPP), Caisse de dépôt et placement du Québec (CDPQ), Ontario Teachers' Pension Plan (OTPP), and Ontario Municipal Employees Retirement System (OMERS).[66] The Big Eight have net investment assets ranging from CAD$64 billion to CAD$265 billion. All eight funds were included in a list of the one hundred largest pension funds, with three of them ranked among the twenty largest funds in the world.[67] These funds have become more and more vocal in the governance of public corporations.[68]

3.5. Proxy Access and Its Dimensions

If shareholder activism can be beneficial for corporations, as SCG predicts, then it is necessary to ask what role (if any) the law should play in facilitating such activism. We must acknowledge that the shareholders seeking to gain power in corporations may be minority shareholders, especially if the corporation is not widely held. Our discussion about reform should include the rights of minority shareholders.

Recall that SCG asks whether shareholders should be able to participate in the governance of corporations. Shareholder participation is believed to be necessary because of the risk of management entrenchment.[69] The ultimate question, and the one that motivates the Bebchuk-Lipton debate, is how much participation is necessary to counter the potential for entrenchment.[70] To deal with the issue, this section explores proposals for increased "proxy access."

(a) Proxy Access

Those who favor "proxy access" argue that shareholders' ability to elect directors should be supplemented by the power to nominate them for election and place them on the same ballot as management's nominees. The intended goal of this reform would be to increase the levels of independence and quality of boards of directors, while providing shareholders with a meaningful say in who is able to become a director.

Current law in Canada, the United States, and the United Kingdom allows shareholders to nominate directors under certain circumstances, with much variation among jurisdictions.[71] In Canada, while there is no statutory right to nominate directors per se, there are three available means by which shareholders can make such nominations. First, they may do so through the shareholder proposal mechanism, which exists independent of the securities-law rules relating to proxy contests and allows any voting shareholder to submit a proposal to the corporation, provided certain conditions are met.[72] Second, shareholders can go through the dissident proxy process.[73] Third, shareholders who own more than 5 percent of the corporation's shares can also requisition a meeting to nominate a director.[74] All three of these mechanisms can be prohibitively expensive, with no guarantee that management will accept the proposal or requisition.

Shareholders in US companies, as in Canada, can submit proposals to the board, provided they have held at least $2,000 or 1 percent of the company's voting securities for at least one year.[75] However, the right is subject to an override of sorts. Rule 14a-8 specifically allows the board to exclude any proposal that "[s]eeks to include a specific individual in the company's proxy materials for election to the board of directors."[76] If a shareholder decides to nominate directors via dissident proxy materials, another obstacle presents itself: under the "bona fide nominee rule," a proxy statement cannot confer the power to vote for its nominee unless that nominee consents to being named on that specific proxy statement and to serving if elected.[77] In practice, because the boards' own nominees very rarely consent to be nominated in shareholder proxy contests, it is not usually possible for shareholders to vote for shareholder nominees alongside management nominees.[78] Unlike in Canada, shareholders have no right to requisition meetings under federal securities or Delaware corporate law (unless such a right is granted to them by the corporation's by-laws).[79]

In 2010, the SEC implemented a controversial proxy access rule intended to make the nomination process more accessible, allowing shareholders with a 3 percent share held continuously for three years to have a nominee included on proxy materials.[80] However, this rule was vacated by the US Court of Appeals for the D.C. Circuit in 2011.[81] A 2016 SEC proposal, not yet adopted, would allow shareholders to vote for a full slate of directors regardless of who nominated them via a "universal ballot" voting card.[82] This rule would make it considerably easier for dissenting shareholders to achieve some representation on the board. Despite the difficulty in enacting policy reforms that increase proxy access, there has been pressure from shareholders for companies to implement proxy access by-laws.[83] As of mid-2017, 60 percent of the S&P 500 companies had implemented such by-laws.[84]

It is easier for shareholders in the United Kingdom to nominate directors, because these boards do not have discretionary authority to exclude binding proposals from proxy materials.[85] Under the UK Companies Act 2006, any shareholder who holds at least 5 percent of the company (unless the firm's by-laws specify a lower percentage) can submit and require circulation of a resolution,[86] and the same shareholders also have the right to require directors to call a general meeting.[87] The United Kingdom does not have the bona fide nominee rule,[88] and resolutions to appoint or remove directors require a simple majority vote.[89] Shareholders are able to influence the corporation through resolutions demanding positive action, including appointment of specific directors.

Some may argue that the law cited above, especially in Canada and the United States, evidences a shareholder-centric bias.[90] However, one may reasonably respond that shareholders' ability to elect directors has little meaning if they do not have a definite say over the precise names that appear on the ballot in the first place. No statutory provision exists that enables them to do that explicitly and directly.[91]

Critics of proxy access may argue that directors nominated by a shareholder will be beholden to the shareholder rather than the corporation as a whole. However, directors have a duty to act in the best interests of the corporation, regardless of who nominated them.[92] Directors continuously face conflicts in the course of discharging their duties, but as fiduciaries, they are obliged by law to rise above such conflicts. To argue that directors nominated by certain shareholders would be unable to rise to the legal standard required of them suggests that these directors, and directors generally, are unable to separate their personal interests from their duty to corporations. Why are shareholder nominees any different from the director population at large, many of whom are employed by or represent related parties, such as controlling shareholders or management?

Critics may further argue that proxy access would allow a shareholder or a group of shareholders to take control of the board over time. Thus, some type of "ceiling" seems reasonable. One proposal is to allow shareholders who hold 3 to 5 percent of the corporation's outstanding shares to have a right to nominate the lesser of three directors or 20 percent of the board.[93] Another possibility is to enable minority shareholders who have held a certain percentage of shares over a certain period of time to name at least one nominee on every slate presented to shareholders at annual shareholder meetings.[94]

These reform proposals may seem far-fetched. But there does not have to be a gap between those who wish to see increased shareholder democracy on the one hand and those who are concerned about the well-being of the corporation on the other.[95] We turn now to consider some of the advantages of increased shareholder democracy for the corporation.

(b) Advantages of Proxy Access for the Corporation

A number of advantages result from proxy access. First, shareholder presence on the board can be an antidote to "groupthink" norms that suppress innovation and meaningful dissent. Some argue that groupthink has been a factor in corporate scandals (for example, Enron) and helps to explain the passivity of corporate boards.[96] It is argued that corporations need the shareholders to supply them with directors who will not hesitate to bring different viewpoints to boardroom tables. The alternative—no direct, nondiscretionary input from shareholders into the nomination process—will do little to dispel apprehension regarding management and board entrenchment, and, more important, will do little to change prevailing corporate governance processes that at times have been at the root of corporate governance failures.

Second, shareholder representation on the board could increase board independence, expertise, and effective risk management. Murphy argues that "shareholder participation in corporate governance can help give the chair [of the board] the independence necessary to carry out an effective leadership role."[97] In addition, greater shareholder participation in the nomination process could help to ensure that the board is properly qualified.[98]

Third, as mentioned in section 3.3 above, studies demonstrate that shareholder activism has led to increases in corporate value, output, and performance.[99] Bebchuk, for example, describes how target companies underperforming during the two years prior to an intervention subsequently recovered in the two years after the intervention, without any evidence of adverse long-term effects.[100] Bebchuk's finding of the positive stock price reaction to interventions in the short and long term suggests that greater shareholder representation and involvement in nominating directors could benefit corporations.

This discussion about shareholder activism is central to SCG. It is the phenomenon that gives rise to SCG itself. SCG suggests that the balance in law is tilted too far in favor of boards. But there are legitimate arguments on both sides of the debate. Ultimately, with regard to proxy access, it is a matter of making shareholders' existing right to elect directors meaningful: what is the point of a right to elect if shareholders do not also have some say in the choice of the person for whom they are voting?

3.6. Conclusion

SCG is by definition imprecise, but it is at least a means to understand the polarizing debate between those who argue in favor of director primacy vis-à-vis shareholder democracy. It refers to a movement rather than a specific state of affairs. The SDS reflects this imprecision. In particular, current law does not evidence unbridled director primacy; shareholders already have a bundle of rights under corporate law, but this bundle is constantly changing, as the next chapter explores.

4

Activism, Wolf Packs, and SCG

4.1. Introduction

Is it possible that SCG might go too far? Recognizing that corporate law seeks to mediate between a corporation's directors and its shareholders by assigning each a distinct set of legal responsibilities and rights,[1] this chapter considers issues that can arise when shareholders have too much power over how a corporation is run.

SCG acknowledges the need to reconsider the historical division between ownership and control in publicly traded corporations.[2] Benefits accrue to investors, and the corporation as a whole, as a result of shareholder activism. The size and sophistication of large institutional investors enable them to monitor management and play a potentially meaningful role in steering the corporation. Smaller shareholders, who individually lack the means to operate as activists, benefit from having these large players protect interests that parallel their own.[3] But while shareholder activism has many economic benefits, it also creates new challenges.

The recent emergence of "wolf packs" is an important case in point. Wolf packs are loose networks of like-minded shareholders (typically hedge funds) that act together to effect change in a corporation without disclosing their collective interest.[4] Just as institutions that own large blocks of a corporation may hold sufficient sway to have a significant impact on the corporation's value, a group of individually smaller blockholders operating in tandem under the direction of a pack leader can have a similar impact.[5]

Wolf packs might most commonly feature alliances between a hedge fund, as lead activist, and one or more fellow institutional

Shareholder-Driven Corporate Governance. Anita Indira Anand, Oxford University Press (2020).

DOI: 10.1093/oso/9780190096533.001.0001

investors. For example, the Canadian Pension Plan Investment Board publicly supported William Ackman's activist campaign at CP Rail in 2012.[6] The tendency of wolf packs to be made up of institutional investors may be explained in part by empirical work relating to wolf packs, which suggests that lead activists may tip off other funds with which they have existing relationships.[7] In other words, wolf packs will typically be made up of "repeat" groups of shareholders.

Wolf packs are able to circumvent disclosure rules typically applied to shareholders that act together by deliberately avoiding being characterized as a "group" for the purposes of US securities laws or as "acting jointly or in concert" under comparable Canadian securities laws.[8] As in a group of prowling wolves, the lead wolf (shareholder) might be visible to its prey, while the other wolves appear only when they are needed.

Building on our discussion of SCG in previous chapters, this chapter examines wolf pack activity as a distinct form of shareholder activism and asks what challenges it presents to legal regimes, particularly in proxy contests and other change-of-control transactions. Changes of control, especially in cases of hostile takeovers, are controversial because they often necessitate a consideration of strategic objectives different from those of the target company's board prior to the takeover.

Wolf packs add an element of controversy, as the pack typically forms before the share price increase that often accompanies a change-of-control transaction, thus allowing its members to take advantage of any appreciation. Wolf packs must overcome the coordination costs and other impediments that smaller shareholders experience in forming de facto blocks, thereby enabling themselves to initiate a proxy contest or a push for sale of the corporation.[9]

Several factors affect wolf pack formation by incentivizing shareholder cooperation and making it easier for shareholders to overcome the costs of coordination and activism. To begin, wolf packs are much more likely to form when large institutional shareholders are present, because these sophisticated, rational institutions are well equipped to coordinate with one another. Corporate and securities laws may facilitate wolf pack formation by explicitly allowing coordination among a small group of shareholders, which has the effect of driving the lead activist to focus its recruitment efforts on larger shareholders. This result is especially pronounced in Canadian capital markets, which are characterized by institutional shareholders that hold sizable positions in public corporations.[10] Mandatory-disclosure rules may also influence wolf pack activity by requiring disclosure whenever a shareholder passes a certain threshold percentage of ownership. The filing of these disclosures tends to bring about an increase in share price, thus incentivizing pack members to snap up shares before the disclosure.

Two hypotheses explaining wolf pack formation currently dominate the nascent academic literature.[11] Coffee and Palia suggest that a lead activist will actively recruit other investors to join the pack before filing disclosure regarding its holdings.[12] By contrast, Brav et al. assert that pack formation is not usually prompted by explicit coordination. Rather, the lead wolf initiates a "coordination game" simply by assuming a particular activist stance, thus incentivizing pack movement.[13] Both of these models—which can be referred to as the explicit-coordination and implicit-coordination models—are informative, but neither is sufficient to explain fully how wolf packs form. The explicit-coordination model rightly concentrates on the timing of pack formation in the regulatory context of disclosure requirements but does not adequately account for the actual mechanics of pack members' decision to band together. Meanwhile, the implicit-coordination model explains this decision but discounts the importance of a lead activist in coordinating the wolf pack.

This chapter pushes the analysis of wolf pack formation further than these two models by isolating conditions in addition to timing that might engender shareholder coordination and considering this phenomenon in connection with the previous chapters' discussion of SCG. It focuses on the concept of investor sophistication, for example, as a contributing element to wolf pack formation. It also highlights the benefits of wolf packs for smaller, less sophisticated shareholders who free-ride on the activism of the lead wolf or shareholder. Finally, it analogizes wolf packs to blockholders generally in terms of the monitoring function that both the blockholder and the lead wolf play.

Another difference between this chapter's arguments and the existing models for wolf pack behavior referred to above is that the latter are predicated on US law and, in particular, the filing of US disclosure triggered at a 5 percent ownership threshold. By contrast, in Canada, shareholders are generally required only to disclose equity holdings in excess of 10 percent.[14] Given that lead activists do not typically acquire a stake greater than 10 percent in connection with their campaigns,[15] wolf packs in Canada can form more easily without disclosure of a lead activist's presence. Wolf packs can therefore exert more influence in the corporate governance of Canadian corporations without having to disclose their holdings.

Section 4.2 examines wolf pack formation and analogizes their behavior to blockholders. That section considers how regulatory features of a given regime, such as Canada, can facilitate wolf pack formation. Section 4.3 takes up the controversial question of how securities regulators should respond to wolf packs. In particular, that section argues that for the purposes of disclosure rules, wolf packs should be treated in the same manner as blockholders (i.e., shareholders that own a large amount of a corporation's shares, usually between 5 and 10 percent, sufficient to influence the corporation's decisions generally). Because blockholders and wolf packs perform similar roles in the corporation, they should be treated as like entities in the eyes of the law. Section 4.4 concludes.

4.2. Wolf Pack Formation and Behavior

Blockholders perform an important monitoring function when they are incentivized to do so (i.e., when the private benefits of monitoring outweigh its costs). Wolf packs are a type of blockholder, and they, too, perform an important monitoring function. Reliable empirical data on the incidence of wolf packs are difficult to obtain, since ungrouped shareholders are not obliged to make disclosures in connection with their collective position.[16] However, a wolf pack will only form when it is able to overcome the free-rider problem and coordination costs identified above, which keep smaller shareholders from monitoring and impede the formation of de facto blocks by networks of smaller shareholders.[17]

According to the explicit-coordination model, Coffee and Palia argue that a lead activist will recruit other investors to join the wolf pack before filing the required disclosure, called a Schedule 13D in the United States (whose equivalent is an early-warning report in Canada).[18] Subsequent members of the pack are rewarded with a riskless arbitrage opportunity in return for their support of the lead activist's agenda. The lead activist tips off the pack's other members before filing its Schedule 13D, which is generally associated with a jump in the share price.[19] As such, the wolf pack is formed before disclosure is made through the explicit coordination efforts of the lead activist. As Bratton notes, although the purchase activity of subsequent members of the pack makes it more expensive for the lead activist to make further purchases in the target corporation, that the lead activist is required to share its gains with other members of the pack does not inhibit the activist from assuming a lead position.[20] Just as members of the wolf pack are careful to avoid "acting jointly or in concert" for the purposes of disclosure rules, they are also careful not to breach insider trading and tipping laws.[21]

Under what we may term an implicit-coordination model, Brav et al. assert that a coordination game drives wolf pack formation, since individual shareholders are incentivized to join wolf packs without explicit coordination by a lead member.[22] Wolf packs arise spontaneously because investors monitor the same corporations at generally the same times. Each "small" independent investor on its own does not have sufficient incentive to monitor and intervene, because the probability of a successful campaign is low and the expected benefits do not outweigh the costs. However, the entry of a large investor, whose position is conveyed to the other small investors through the filing of disclosure when it passes the 5 percent ownership threshold, operates as a catalytic event that increases the expected probability of a successful intervention and in turn motivates small investors to join the intervention and thus form a wolf pack. The rational self-interest of the members of the wolf pack is sufficient for the wolf pack to form on the basis of implicit coordination *after* the lead activist discloses its position to the market.

As mentioned, these models are predicated on US law and in particular the filing of a Schedule 13D, which is triggered at a 5 percent ownership threshold. In other jurisdictions such as Canada, shareholders are generally only required to disclose equity holdings in excess of 10 percent.[23] Because of this rule and others,[24] lead activists do not typically acquire a stake greater than 10 percent in connection with their campaigns,[25] meaning that wolf packs in Canada can form without the disclosure of a lead activist's presence.

A number of variables affect the viability of shareholder coordination in the form of wolf pack activity. For instance, wolf packs are more likely to act upon widely held corporations than controlled corporations, in which voting control resides with the founder. In such cases, the wolf pack will always be outvoted by the controlling shareholder, unless the controlling shareholder forms part of the wolf pack.[26] As a result, a proxy contest, or the threat of a proxy contest, may be an ineffective means of agitating for change in the corporation. In Canada, many public corporations are dominated by a controlling shareholder[27] who is often the founder or the founder's family.[28] This tendency may mean that the Canadian capital market is less amenable to wolf pack activity than that of the United States, where corporations are more commonly widely held.

Another important factor is the presence of an institutional shareholder, without which wolf pack formation is extremely unlikely.[29] The institution may or may not take on the role of lead activist. Regardless, its sophistication will allow it to fulfill a monitoring function, a byproduct of which is to provide subsequent members' an opportunity to free-ride on the wolf pack's efforts. In Canada, corporations' share ownership tends to be dominated by larger institutional holders.[30] In some exceptional cases, pension funds, which are not typically activists,[31] may also join and form a collective to defend against a change-of-control transaction.[32]

Wolf packs, by definition, will have a leader who must bear the costs of monitoring up front before persuading other shareholders to join the wolf pack. It is unlikely that the lead activist will begin a campaign for governance reform where any gains are likely to be modest. Rather, the lead activist would likely need to present a plan for the corporation that involves a change of control. The lead activist is willing to bear these monitoring costs up front because the likelihood of a wolf pack's achieving at least one of its intended outcomes is significantly higher than that of an individual activist.[33] As a result, the expected benefits of monitoring rise relative to the costs.

We must remember that the lead activist's position likely sends a signal to other investors. By the time the lead contacts other shareholders, it will have fulfilled at least a portion of its self-imposed monitoring function, thereby allowing subsequent members of the wolf pack to free-ride on its efforts. Because the institutional investors that tend to hold sizable positions in Canadian corporations are not generally activists, they may benefit from a lead activist who has borne (or will bear) the costs of monitoring up front.

Wolf pack formation may occur more easily in some jurisdictions. Coffee notes, for instance, that the wolf pack strategy is not common in the United Kingdom or Australia. Comparing those jurisdictions with the American context, Coffee suggests that the difference could be a consequence of the much shorter window period in those countries between crossing the ownership threshold and the filing of mandatory disclosure. The shorter window period means less opportunity for informed trading and thus less short-term profit for wolf pack members.[34]

Unlike in the United Kingdom, securities law in Canada likely facilitates wolf pack formation. In particular, the current rules relating to shareholder coordination may assist this kind of activism. Shareholders can be incentivized to join a wolf pack because of the opportunity for riskless profit provided by the spike in share price that tends to follow the filing of an early-warning report.[35] Even without filing the report, the lead activist can manufacture a comparable share price appreciation by notifying potential members of the wolf pack of its intentions to initiate a proxy contest or agitate for a sale of the target.[36] Indeed, the threat of a proxy contest is perhaps more credible under Canadian securities laws than in other jurisdictions, because these laws allow a dissident shareholder to wage a proxy contest relatively inexpensively, without the need to prepare and mail a proxy circular to other shareholders under the public-broadcast exemption.[37] In addition, under the fifteen-shareholder proxy solicitation exemption, a dissident shareholder is permitted to solicit proxies from a limited number of shareholders without having to prepare and mail a proxy circular.[38]

The factors discussed above have a significant impact on wolf pack formation, and the conditions identified may be necessary to allow wolf packs to be meaningfully active. First, the corporation must be widely held rather than being controlled by its founder. Second, the presence of a controlling shareholder or institutional investor may be necessary in order to provide the monitoring of the corporation's management that is an essential first step toward collective activism. Third, there must be a lead activist prepared to absorb the costs that allow other institutions or smaller investors to free-ride, thereby potentially broadening the scope of support for the wolf pack's intervention. The fourth factor relates to the legal regime in place. Rules that lessen disclosure and alleviate the burden of filing proxy materials facilitate wolf pack formation, as discussed in the next section.

4.3. Legal Regime

There are no formal rules relating to wolf packs per se, but their coordinated nature implicates rules relating to proxy solicitation, early-warning reporting, and possibly insider trading. While wolf packs form loose networks of investors, they generally seek to accumulate a base of support without triggering the shareholder disclosure obligations that would arise if the group's aggregate position exceeded certain ownership thresholds. This section examines competing considerations—including wolf packs' likely preferences—regarding the prevailing legal regime and considers whether changes to this regime are warranted, particularly in a regulatory system that accommodates and facilitates SCG.

(a) A Rationale for Disclosure Requirements

One rationale for securities disclosure laws, including blockholder disclosures, relates to price efficiency:[39] public issuers are mandated to disclose material information so that stock prices accurately reflect all such material information.[40] There is also a strand of literature that calls for mandatory disclosure on the basis that such disclosure reduces agency costs between managers and shareholders; disclosure makes monitoring easier and decreases the likelihood that managers use corporate assets for self-interested purposes.[41]

Wolf packs, like other activist investors, generally prefer less disclosure to more, likely because of the constraints that disclosure places on their behavior.[42] A loose disclosure regime allows wolf packs to outflank corporate defenses, such as poison pills, which are triggered when a shareholder or group of shareholders passes an ownership threshold prescribed by the pill. It becomes impossible to trigger the pill when the size of the wolf pack's position remains unknown.[43]

Less disclosure also allows activists to leverage their superior information regarding the size of the pack when engaging the target board.[44] Furthermore, empirical studies have shown that Schedule 13D disclosure is associated with positive abnormal share price appreciation.[45] It therefore becomes more expensive for a shareholder to purchase shares in a corporation after filing this disclosure; efficient markets force large shareholders to buy at prices that reflect their own price impact after the filing, which erodes their returns.[46]

While SCG posits the importance of taking the positive effects of shareholder activism into account, the appropriate regulatory response to wolf packs is one that considers both the benefits and the potential hazards of this kind of activism. On the one hand, a legal regime that makes it easier for wolf packs to form and requires less disclosure regarding their investments renders it more likely that the monitoring benefits engendered by large blockholders will materialize. As discussed in the previous chapters, such monitoring benefits all shareholders and is one of the cornerstones of SCG.

On the other hand, however, many investors may find the mere presence or identity of a wolf pack to be material in making investment decisions, which means that the information contained in mandatory disclosures may have a significant impact on securities prices. A lenient disclosure regime for wolf packs may allow them to accumulate de facto control blocks without paying other shareholders a control premium, thus facilitating "creeping takeovers."[47] It is also well recognized that blockholders can potentially extract private benefits of control, which can impose costs on other shareholders.[48] Forcing wolf packs to disclose their positions protects non–wolf pack shareholders against both of these risks. These concerns are relevant to (but distinct from) the so-called short-termism that hedge funds may exhibit when they are more committed to short-term value maximization rather than managers' long-term strategies for the corporation.

In the face of these competing arguments, is more or less disclosure regarding wolf pack formation appropriate? The norms of SCG, as well as the mandate of securities regulators, demand protection for nonactivist shareholders where the actions of activists, including wolf packs, threaten to impose costs upon them without benefit. Notwithstanding the potential benefits of allowing more wolf pack activity, regulators should treat wolf packs as blockholders and require them to disclose their positions.

(b) The Legal Regimes in Canada and the United States

Under Canadian securities law, disclosure rules affecting the formation and disclosure of wolf packs generally fall within the blockholder disclosure rules for early-warning reporting.[49] The early-warning system requires acquirers who hold more than 10 percent of an issuer's outstanding securities to disclose their positions to the market in a promptly filed news release and early-warning report and to file additional disclosures upon any additional 2 percent purchase of the issuer's securities.[50] This system deems shares purchased by those who act "jointly or in concert" with an acquirer to have also been purchased by the acquirer, aggregating their collective holdings to determine whether the 10 percent threshold has been crossed.

For instance, an acquirer in Canada with a 7 percent stake in a given issuer would be required to file an early-warning report if it were acting jointly or in concert with another shareholder holding a 4 percent stake. Determining whether two parties are acting jointly or in concert with each other is a question of fact,[51] and there is limited case law addressing the issue.[52] Of course, how courts—or the regulator in the form of tribunal decisions and policy directives—interpret the breadth of this statutory language will have a significant impact on how wolf packs can form and the nature and timing of their disclosure obligations.

As mentioned above, the rules governing wolf pack disclosure in the United States fall under the "beneficial ownership" rules in section 13(d) of the Securities and Exchange Act of 1934. The SEC defines "beneficial ownership" as any person who indirectly or directly holds voting or investment power in a corporation.[53] Section 13(d) mandates that when a beneficial owner acquires 5 percent or more of a company's shares, that owner is required to disclose this ownership, along with additional information relating to group membership and the purpose of the purchase, to the commission within ten days of crossing the 5 percent threshold through the filing of a Schedule 13D.[54] A beneficial owner may be able to forgo filing a Schedule 13D and instead file a short-form version under section 13(g) if the shares have not been acquired for the purpose of changing or influencing control of the company.[55] If the shareholder acquires ownership of 10 percent or more, then it becomes subject to section 16, which has its own disclosure requirements as well as additional implications for the shareholder.[56]

Section 13(d)(3) relates specifically to wolf packs by including partnerships, joint ventures, and groups within the definition of a "person." The act defines a group as two or more people who are acting together for the purpose of buying, acquiring, or selling a company's shares.[57]

What constitutes a group in US securities law differs slightly from Canada's "jointly and in concert" criterion. In the United

States, courts look at whether the parties are acting together "in the furtherance of a common objective."[58] The case law also indicates that the agreement can be formal or informal and does not have to be in writing, but there must be evidence of some understanding between the parties to work in tandem toward achieving a common goal.[59] Thus, wolf packs try to avoid being categorized as a group under this definition so as to avoid their shares being aggregated under section 13(d). By avoiding forming a "group," the wolf pack can delay the need to file a Schedule 13D. However, if a court finds the wolf pack to constitute a "group," then all members can be sued for alleged disclosure violations.[60] A 2015 press release by the SEC highlights how seriously the SEC takes the enforcement of beneficial ownership disclosure. In three separate cases concerning section 13(d), the commission ordered civil monetary penalties and cease-and-desist orders against the parties for failing to comply with disclosure requirements.[61]

(c) The Need for Wolf Pack Disclosure

Wolf packs are effectively blockholders. Shareholders form de facto blocks to exert influence on the corporation in much the same manner as a blockholder but are able to avoid disclosure rules simply by avoiding the characterization of their behavior as joint action. Thus, wolf packs should be regulated like blockholders. That is, they should be subject to early-warning reporting when their collective interest rises above 10 percent, just as a blockholder is subject to early-warning reporting when its individual interest crosses that threshold.[62] Investors should not need to make decisions in the absence of material information, such as the existence of a wolf pack. Although it is true that blockholders fulfill an important monitoring role in the corporation, the regulator has presumably already weighed this benefit against the need for investors to make investment decisions with access to material information regarding blockholders. If this policy choice has been made in respect of blockholders, then the law's treatment of wolf packs should be no different.

Central to the analogy between blockholders and wolf packs is the concept of "acting jointly and in concert." Interpretation of this statutory language dictates whether wolf packs will be subject to the same disclosure rules as blockholders; a narrow understanding of what qualifies as joint action allows individual members of the wolf pack to consider only their respective interest for the purposes of passing disclosure thresholds. For instance, in the US context, the Second Circuit held that three shareholders were not acting as a "group," even though one shareholder "was a well-known raider and all three discussed amongst themselves how to improve the value of the target company."[63] In light of the foregoing analysis concerning the costs that wolf packs can impose on other shareholders, a regulatory regime is seriously deficient if it is insensitive to the *coordinated* nature of wolf pack activity. For this reason, the concept of "acting jointly and in concert" should be interpreted and applied broadly to cover a wide range of communication and behaviors associated with wolf pack formation. In particular, tipping by the lead member of the wolf pack to other investors regarding the lead member's plans in relation to the target should qualify as joint conduct.

Although courts are afforded broad latitude with respect to the remedies they may impose upon a breach of securities regulation, the judicial posture has traditionally been one of restraint. As one court recently stated, "the surgery should be done with a scalpel and not a battle axe."[64] In one of the few cases dealing with the scope of what behavior qualifies as "acting jointly or in concert" in the context of a proposed proxy contest, the court refused to bar the wolf pack's members from voting their shares despite holding that the wolf pack breached its disclosure obligations; instead, the court ordered the wolf pack to make appropriate disclosures regarding its joint action and delayed the annual general meeting of the shareholders until the shareholders had adequate time to review such disclosures.[65] Future decisions should consider that wolf packs should not be permitted special status in the "acting jointly or in concert" analysis, especially in light of the potentially weak remedies imposed on them for noncompliance.[66]

Of course, underlying the foregoing discussion of the relationship between disclosure and wolf packs is a potential link between wolf pack formation to insider trading and tipping. The chance at riskless profit engendered by wolf packs—based on the relationships between and among specific institutional shareholders—seems to run contrary to the policy animating insider trading and tipping laws, which is to protect "investor confidence in the marketplace as a level playing field."[67] If it is the case that rules make illegal tipping by persons or companies contemplating takeover bids[68] because of the premium such bids typically command and that the announcement of proxy contests usually results in a similar share price appreciation,[69] then we can legitimately question why one type of behavior is captured by tipping rules while another is not. Securities regulators should consider whether tipping rules should apply to persons or companies contemplating proxy contests, another form of change of control.

Thus, a regulatory regime that accommodates and facilitates SCG must also attend to the potential dangers that emerge when small blockholders act collectively as a wolf pack. This is normatively consistent with the regulatory approach to SCG, because its goal is to strike a balance between the interests of those shareholders who operate as activists and those who hold shares without playing such an active role in the corporation.

4.4. Conclusion

It is challenging to ascertain precise figures on the incidence of wolf packs.[70] Nevertheless, this chapter represents a first step toward understanding the circumstances that engender their formation and the motivations that drive the behavior of their members. Wolf packs occupy the role of a blockholder in the corporation but without the same disclosure obligations that blockholders are required to observe. While a legal regime that facilitates wolf pack formation, including a narrow concept of "acting jointly or in concert," may make it easier for shareholders to monitor management and thus reduce agency costs in changes of control, these benefits should not come at the price of deficient disclosure. If a sound disclosure system is the cornerstone of securities regulation, then novel tactics aimed at circumventing that system—especially when analogous shareholders are caught by it—should be more comprehensively regulated.

Wolf packs offer an example of the potential for conflicts of interest between shareholders in a system that accommodates shareholder activism in its many forms. The next chapter addresses the possibility of conflicts of interest between shareholders and management, a potentiality to which SCG is largely a response.

5
Multiple-Voting Share Structures

5.1. Introduction

Shareholder-driven corporate governance, the central concept of this book, provides us with an analytical standpoint from which to comprehend and critique certain hot-button issues in corporate governance. Specifically, these issues involve divergences of interest between those who own the corporation (shareholders) and those who control it. Chapter 4 addressed a specific situation in which interests can diverge among shareholders: one group of investors takes up the wolf pack strategy, while fellow shareholders may have interests contrary to those of the pack. Such conflicts produce costs for one or both groups, often referred to as principal conflict costs." [1]

This chapter examines multiple-voting share (MVS) structures, which allow insiders to control governance, thus building the potential for conflicts of interest into the corporation's own rules. When a firm goes public using an MVS structure, it issues two or more classes of shares, one to the public and another to insiders (typically founders, promoters, management, private investors, or board members).[2] The shares that are issued publicly have limited voting rights, while the class issued to insiders carries more voting rights, allowing the insiders to control the company without owning a majority of shares of the firm.[3] This corporate structure disrupts the one-to-one ratio of votes to shares that, in non-MVS firms, gives minority shareholders a voice that is on par with other shareholders: one share held equals one vote that the shareholders can cast.

Shareholder-Driven Corporate Governance. Anita Indira Anand, Oxford University Press (2020).

DOI: 10.1093/oso/9780190096533.001.0001

By allowing issuers to accept public capital without relinquishing control of the corporation, MVS structures raise important questions relating to the rights of investors. Regulators in jurisdictions around the world, including the United States, Canada, France, and Japan, are examining these structures and asking how best to respond to them. Meanwhile, a growing group of investors refuse to purchase MVSs as a matter of principle. Clearly, MVS structures have policy implications that warrant further discussion. This chapter aims to contribute to this policy debate by examining the dissonance between MVS structures and the normative concept of SCG. It argues that MVSs create a power structure in which outside shareholders carry a disproportionate share of the firm's economic risk relative to their ability to influence its governance. An MVS structure deprives these shareholders of their ex ante rights by undercutting the efficacy of the vote, leaving the subordinate shareholders unable to affect change in the corporation.[4]

Section 5.2 explains and critiques the arguments put forward in defense of MVS structures. Section 5.3 considers the rights of minority shareholders and explains how MVSs tend to exacerbate the already disadvantageous position of these shareholders. Section 5.4 outlines three policy recommendations for the regulation of MVSs that would serve to protect the interests of minority and subordinate shareholders, namely, mandatory sunset clauses, disclosure of shareholder voting, and buyout protections. Section 5.5 concludes.

5.2. Deconstructing MVS Structures

While MVS structures are prevalent in the United States, they are even more so in Canada.[5] Their popularity suggests that issuers as well as investors have an appetite for this type of capital structure.[6] A number of well-known US companies, including Berkshire Hathaway, Alphabet (formerly Google), and Facebook, have MVS structures. Indeed, MVS structures seem to be gaining popularity among firms going public. For example, recently, Cara and Stingray have gone public using this structure in Canada. Shopify made a $100 million initial public offering (IPO) in Toronto and New York, offering the public Class A shares with one vote per share, while company founders and insiders received Class B shares which entitled owners to ten votes per share. FitBit, Box, and a division of Alibaba have also adopted MVS structures.[7]

Historically, Canadian firms (for example, Bombardier, Fairfax, and Rogers) issued MVSs in order to preserve family or founder control while allowing the firm to gain access to capital in public equity markets. Family or founding members would retain voting control while the restricted shares were offered to the public.[8] This is the most prominent argument in favor of MVS structures: by localizing control with the founders, they prevent outsiders from easily taking over the firm without the controlling shareholder's cooperation.[9] Advocates also argue that MVS structures allow the founders to focus on long-term value creation and motivate them to make firm-specific investments in their own human capital.[10] Whereas investors may not hold their securities for the long term, founders and managers are more likely to do so and are therefore be better placed to make decisions in the firm's long-term interest. MVSs protect the founders from the demands of ordinary shareholders, allowing them more freedom to grow the corporation.[11]

One consequence of the protective power of MVS structures is that they dissuade potential suitors who would otherwise be willing to pay a premium for shares and who may in fact be better able to run the business, which would be a boon to all but the controlling shareholders. MVSs also insulate management and the board for time immemorial, leaving minority shareholders exposed to decisions that undermine their economic interests. The separation of ownership and control in the MVS context thus has the potential to increase agency costs significantly.

In response to the apparent disadvantages of these corporate structures from the perspective of subordinate shareholders, many scholars defend MVS structures on the grounds that investors should choose for themselves whether such structures are acceptable to them. As Stephen Bainbridge notes:

> Public investors who don't want lesser voting rights stock simply won't buy it. Those who are willing to purchase it presumably will be compensated by a lower per share price than full voting rights stock would command and/or by a higher dividend rate. In any event, assuming full disclosure, they become shareholders knowing that they will have lower voting rights than the insiders and having accepted as adequate whatever trade-off is offered by the firm in recompense.[12]

I refer to this line of thinking as the caveat emptor argument: investors purchase at their own risk based on the information available to them in the form of mandated disclosures, which they can find in firms' (often unwieldy) prospectuses and proxy circulars.

Of course, there is a price at which prospective investors are willing to accept negative firm characteristics, including agency costs and bad corporate governance. Zingales found that voting shares commanded an 82 percent premium over nonvoting shares in Italy.[13] So while MVS structures have their governance weaknesses, there is, as a practical matter, a price at which the market seems willing to accept these drawbacks. The same principle applies to inferior shares that carry a vote but carry little or no real power.

The caveat emptor argument for MVS structures is rooted in the free choice of investors: if investors find MVSs unappealing from an investment standpoint, they simply need not invest. If they decide after the fact that MVSs are unacceptable, they can sell their shares. Meanwhile, those who do decide to purchase subordinate shares in the MVS firm can free-ride on the monitoring done by the founding/controlling shareholder(s).[14] This line of reasoning is consistent with the contractarian model of the corporation, discussed in chapter 2, which has long dominated corporate-law theory:[15] if the corporation is merely a nexus of contracts, then capital structure is simply one aspect of the contractual relationship between the shareholder and the firm. If investors do not like MVSs, nothing is forcing them to enter into these contractual relationships in the first place.

The caveat emptor argument is not a sound basis for securities regulatory policy given the mandates of securities regulators across the globe to protect the interests of investors and to maintain healthy capital markets. This mandate is a response to the complex realities of the marketplace, which are such that the investment decisions of supposedly rational investors are not always sufficient to protect the interests of the investing public. Accordingly, securities regulation places an "overlay" on top of the fundamentally contractual relationships between issuers and shareholders. This overlay consist of rules premised not on the concept of "buyer beware" but on the need for meaningful investor protection.

Regulators have an obligation to make policies that protect investors, over and above the protection that investors afford themselves by consulting disclosures and deciding whether or not to invest.[16] These bodies therefore cannot overlook corporate structures that prevent shareholders from participating in corporate decision-making. Regulators' obligation to the public interest may mean that they should consider prohibiting MVSs, which effectively create inequality as between minority shareholders and insiders in corporate decision-making. Prohibiting MVSs could be efficient; Amoako-Adu et al. found that elimination of the MVS structures increases stock prices and improves the liquidity of the stock.[17]

To better understand the effect of MVS structures on investors' interests, the next section provides an analysis of the rights of minority shareholders in general and subordinate shareholders in MVS firms in particular. The presence of MVSs undermines existing accountability mechanisms enshrined in corporate law, thus allowing agency costs to proliferate.

5.3. The Role of Minority Shareholders

Corporate law is often dominated by a tension between the rights and responsibilities of two groups of stakeholders in the corporation: the board of directors on the one hand and the corporation's shareholders on the other. The debate about MVSs is, at its root, about the place of minority shareholders in the corporation. The statutory duty to oversee the corporation and to chart its course while acting in its best interests rests solely with the board of directors.[18] But corporate statutes also embody a principle of majority rule, which provides that the shareholders, not the board of directors or management, should have recourse in the face of a wrong done to the corporation.[19] For example, a majority of shareholders elect the directors, appoint the auditors, approve the financial statements, and push through fundamental changes in the corporation.[20]

Shareholders' rights under corporate law serve as the means by which shareholders may protect their own interests. Some of these rights operate ex ante, allowing shareholders to participate to some degree in the decision-making process, including the rights to approve financial statements, appoint auditors, submit proposals (which may include director nominations),[21] and requisition meetings.[22] Others are ex post rights. These include the "fraud on the minority" cause of action,[23] the dissent and appraisal rights,[24] and the uniquely Canadian oppression remedy.[25] As discussed in chapter 3, the rights available to shareholders are a long way from providing them with sufficient means of protecting their own interests.

Minority shareholders are in a somewhat vulnerable position in any corporation, regardless of whether the firm has an MVS structure. Ultimately subject to the will of the majority, they may face economic loss as a result of decisions by the majority shareholders and/or the board, over which they themselves had no control. Quite apart from the problematic division of power between boards and shareholders, minority shareholders always face the additional risk of abuses by more powerful shareholders, particularly in a controlled corporation. Their relative vulnerability is exacerbated by a corporate statute that is based on the principle of majority rule.[26] MVSs complicate majority rule by dividing control from ownership. Rather than being subject to the rule of the majority, the corporation's governance falls into the hands of an individual or small group who owns a minority of equity but represents a majority of possible votes. The result is that the limited powers that they would otherwise have as minority shareholders become eroded even further.

When a single MVS shareholder or group of shareholders with a minority share holds enough voting power to decide any given question, other shareholders' voting rights become practically meaningless. Of course, the subordinate shareholders still get to vote, but these votes have little or no power against the superior power of the MVS. As a consequence, these shareholders are practically unable to benefit from their ex ante rights, which become meaningless despite the disproportionate economic risk that the inferior shareholders bear.

Thus, MVS structures insulate management, the board, and controlling shareholders.[27] Because there is no fiduciary duty as among shareholders, this structure leaves subordinate shareholders without recourse, unable to challenge corporate leadership.[28] Any benefits of MVS structures do not necessarily accrue to all shareholders. Rather, MVSs favor insiders who have fewer checks on self-dealing (e.g., via largely unfettered ability to define executive pay, bonuses, and stock option plans).[29] MVSs potentially allow senior officers and directors to shirk their duties and/or divert profits. This is especially troubling in light of recent empirical work indicating that managers actively seek ownership of their corporations in ranges typically associated with entrenchment, which suggests a revealed preference on their part to remain in control.[30] MVSs offer them a built-in measure of entrenchment without the economic risk they would bear by purchasing shares themselves.

Some may argue that even if minority shareholders lose their ex ante rights in the face of MVS structures, this loss is not a serious problem, because these same shareholders' ex post rights remain intact, as do their common-law private rights of action.[31] This argument is flawed, because at the moment when ex post remedies become available, the damage has already been done. Furthermore, litigation is costly. A bad transaction is unlikely to be fixed ex post, suggesting that a decline in the firm's share price is possible.

5.4. Reforming MVS Structures

There are legitimate reasons to be concerned about governance in MVS firms. These structures insulate management and the board, whose members may (or may not) act in the long-term best interests of the corporation. Insiders are subject to fewer checks on self-dealing and exercise an unfettered ability to define executive pay, bonuses, and stock option plans. Defenders of MVSs may argue, in accordance with the caveat emptor argument discussed above, that issues pertaining to governance in MVS firms are irrelevant because the subordinate shareholders are not "forced" to carry the risk of weak governance; they can refuse to invest in MVS firms if they do not wish to bear the nonparticipatory risk inherent in these firms. They may argue that such unhappy investors should negotiate the terms of their contract prior to buying into the IPO when they could seek a sunset clause and other material governance protections.[32] But as Daines and Klausner have shown, the "terms" of the IPO are not negotiated and in fact provide little information to the market.[33] In other words, private ordering does not ensure that the subordinate shareholders' interests are protected on an ongoing basis. The insufficiency of private ordering is the normative starting point for SCG, which is the conceptual underpinning of the reform proposals set out below.

(a) Fixed-Term Sunset Clause with Mandatory Vote

Sunset provisions warrant serious consideration.[34] Their rationale is sound: subordinate shareholders' interests may be abused when the corporation makes consistent non-value-maximizing decisions, an incumbent's performance declines, or less talented individuals take control of the company.[35] A sunset provision would mitigate this risk by barring perpetual MVS structures unless subordinate shareholders agree to maintain the structure. The sunset should be in place for a limited term unless further majority of the minority shareholder approval is obtained for the MVSs.

Even the most ardent advocates of MVSs should agree with this reform proposal. After all, if MVSs allow firms to achieve long-term goals that are value-enhancing for all shareholders, superior and subordinate shareholders alike will vote to extend the MVS structure so the talented managers can stay in control. Sunset provisions subject to an extension vote allow firms to reap the purported benefits of an MVS structure while preventing the entrenchment of unexceptional management many years after the initial justification (and investor support) for the MVS structure has dissipated. It was through such a vote, though not in the context of a sunset provision, that Fairfax Financial kept its founder Prem Watsa in place for a defined period of time in accordance with the wishes of minority shareholders.[36]

One could argue that mandatory sunsets might be unnecessary if the MVSs eventually result in an inefficient structure. The superior shareholder could then simply be bought out in a transaction in which the surplus created by the move from a less efficient structure to a more efficient structure is shared between the superior shareholder and the subordinate shareholders. In other words, it may seem that private ordering can accomplish mid-course changes in a firm's governing structure, again making a mandatory sunset unnecessary.[37]

In response to this argument, one must appreciate the potential for abuse in the buyout of the founder. The controversial Magna case in Canada presents an important example of a transaction that could well be called abusive of subordinate shareholders.[38] Magna purchased all MVSs belonging to founder Frank Stronach, constituting 0.6 percent of the equity but 66 percent of the voting rights, in exchange for 9 million subordinate voting shares totaling USD$300 million.[39] The transaction diluted the holdings of the subordinate shareholders and enabled Stronach to be paid a 1,800 percent premium of the trading value of the Class B MVSs. These shareholders were asked to choose the lesser of two evils. On the one hand, if they voted against the transaction, they would be signaling their desire to maintain the status quo in which the superior shareholder and founder controlled the company while holding 0.6 percent of the equity. On the other hand, if they voted for the transaction, they would approve the collapse of the firm's MVS structure and the firm's repurchase of the equity held by a founder who had historically extracted significant private benefits of control. The caveat, however, was that the total consideration to be paid for this transaction to occur was exorbitant.

The choice faced by subordinate shareholders in the Magna case suggests that the greater the private benefits that the founder extracts from a corporation with MVS, the higher the premium that will be paid to extricate the corporation from the founder. Indeed, the board's decision to proceed with the transaction may heighten the incentive for a superior shareholder to increase its private benefits in order to extort a greater premium for the collapse of an MVS structure. This is the power of the despot that the founder can exert.[40]

Stronach's 1,800 percent premium was exorbitant in comparison with both market value and the typical price range that would be paid to eliminate a controlling shareholder.[41] In the face of an astoundingly high premium, the processes that the Magna board and special committee followed warranted close scrutiny and ultimately were inadequate.[42] The special committee did not obtain a fairness opinion and valuation, and the board did not make a recommendation to shareholders. Over and above the absence of these procedural safeguards, the special committee concluded that the transaction had positive benefits for Magna, without assuring itself that it was positive for the subordinate shareholders.[43] The question must be asked: if a board refuses to make a recommendation, and no valuation or fairness opinion is provided, how is it that the minority shareholders are to arrive at an informed opinion that underpins their position and ultimately their vote? Process becomes strikingly important.

(b) Disclosure of Shareholder Voting

When shareholders vote, they can signal dissent or approval of the way the firm is governed. Management may act on these signals even when the results are nonbinding.[44] For example, the United Kingdom became the first country to require that shareholders be given an advisory vote on board pay, which subsequently led to more significant dialogue between shareholders and management and tangible changes to executive pay. Specifically, after this requirement was implemented, executive compensation only rose by 5 to 6 percent in 2006, which was a sharp reduction from the average 14 percent increases in the preceding five years. Indeed, Iliev et al.

conducted a study of 8,160 firms across forty-three countries and found that high rates of dissenting votes from outside shareholders led to higher rates of director turnover and more withdrawals from mergers and acquisitions deals.[45] Their study was consistent with previous empirical research indicating that high dissenting-vote percentages are often followed by corporate governance changes in the following year.[46]

Thus, in the context of MVS firms, requiring the separation and disclosure of subordinate and controlling shareholder vote counts likely encourages greater accountability. It could place pressure on management to change bad behavior. This requirement is similar to the "comply or explain" approach in the United Kingdom, which similarly applies soft pressure on corporations to comply with best-practices recommendations voluntarily.[47] Without such disclosure, one cannot tell how shareholders unaffiliated with the controlling shareholder voted, potentially giving a false sense of support for the management team. By mandating disclosure of controlling and subordinate voting results separately, subordinate shareholders can express their dissatisfaction with the status quo and benefit from the potential disciplining effects that come the disclosed results.

(c) Buyout Protections

The Magna transaction suggests that the process under which buyouts occur is substantively important to the subordinate shareholders. Ensuring that these shareholders are adequately protected in the context of the buyout of the founder is difficult and is an area in which private ordering should yield to the mandate of securities regulators, who, in their role as protectors of investors and the public interest, should be concerned with both process and substance in the buyout of an MVS founder.[48]

Canadian law already requires independent valuations and majority of minority security-holder approvals for specific types of transactions, such as issuer bids, insider bids, business combinations, and related party transactions.[49] In a buyout of the founder, minority shareholders must be provided with a formal, independent valuation of the proposed transaction at the offerer's expense.[50] In addition, securities regulation should specifically mandate that the board form a special committee of independent directors and make a recommendation on the transaction to the subordinate shareholders.[51]

While US securities law contains little regulation relating specifically to MVS structures,[52] regulators in some jurisdictions seem to be moving toward greater regulation. In Canada, the OSC issued guidance regarding minority shareholders in conflict-of-interest transactions, perhaps in response to concerns arising from the Magna transaction.[53] The OSC isolates several key areas for its review of material conflict transactions, namely, timely formation of special committees, a broad committee mandate, independence of special committee members, overreliance on fairness opinions, and considerations of the best interests of both the corporation and its minority shareholders.[54] These reforms are needed, but why do regulators choose "guidance" as opposed to mandatory law?

5.5. Conclusion

SCG reveals an ongoing shift in corporate governance, one that assigns greater participatory rights to shareholders. In the rise of MVS structures, we see a counterpoint to this general trend, with founders resisting the power of investors to change corporate governance. Arguments against MVSs hark back to a broader debate about legal protections for minority shareholders and the role of securities commissions. Central to the securities regulation mandate is the concept of the public interest coupled with investor protection. Indeed, securities regulation places a layer of regulatory considerations over and above the contract that shareholders have entered into with the corporation. The "public interest" has traditionally meant more than shareholders' reasonable expectations and the fairness of the transaction to the shareholders at issue. It has involved a consideration of market integrity, confidence in the capital markets, and specific and general deterrence in terms of sanctions.

Admittedly, investors are not a homogeneous group. The investor protection mandate therefore carries with it some ambiguity with regard to who should be the target group in any given instance. Yet the regulator has a distinct role to play in ensuring that all shareholders (not just majority shareholders) are protected. A first step in doing so would be to focus on the poor governance inherent in MVS structures. If one of the benefits of going public is the ability to access equity from both inside and outside shareholders, then one of the burdens must surely be to place these shareholders on an equal footing with one another.

6

Shareholders and Takeover Bids: Revisiting the Poison Pill

6.1. Introduction

Should law be amended to account for SCG? A useful case study is in change-of-control transactions. The board's power to make decisions on behalf of the company takes on additional importance during a takeover bid, when the directors hold the firm's future in their hands. At the same time, board members' jobs may be on the line, which can amplify their incentive to entrench themselves. As previous chapters have argued, board entrenchment is a possibility, which in turn creates costs for the shareholders, as the corporation is no longer being run strictly with a view to value maximization.

When a company's board is faced with an unwanted acquisition proposal, it may seek to resist the takeover on the grounds that it is not in the firm's best interests. One of the means by which the board may do so is by instituting a shareholder rights plan, or "poison pill." The basic function of the pill is to make the company more expensive to take over, thus creating a disincentive for the bidder.[1] In the most common version of this defensive move, the triggering of the pill allows all shareholders except the bidder to purchase new shares at a discount, thus diluting the old shares and increasing the bidder's costs.[2]

Canadian law and US law differ in their rules regarding poison pills. Canadian law does not allow the pill to be used by a board to stop a takeover outright. Instead, it historically provided time for the target board to negotiate with the bidder to enhanced the

Shareholder-Driven Corporate Governance. Anita Indira Anand, Oxford University Press (2020).

DOI: 10.1093/oso/9780190096533.001.0001

bid price, to solicit competing bids, or to propose an alternative to its shareholders.[3] Without either a higher offer from the bidder or an alternative coming forward, case law stated that "the pill must go,"[4] and the original bidder could proceed with its proposed acquisition transaction.[5] By contrast, boards in the United States can use the pill to stop a transaction; US boards can "just say no."[6] The poison pill is not prevalent in the United Kingdom, where its adoption has generally been viewed as a breach of the director's fiduciary duty.[7]

Recent regulatory responses to poison pills demonstrate a shift toward SCG. While these changes are not perfect, they show that the concepts underlying SCG are receiving greater attention from regulators in the takeover-bid context. In 2015, after years of difficult negotiations and failed attempts, the Canadian Securities Administrators (CSA) proposed a new framework for the regulation of takeover bids.[8] These new rules were adopted, largely unchanged, in 2016.[9] The framework contains the most significant reforms to the takeover-bid regime in Canada in decades.[10] Under the new regime, takeover bids have an irrevocable 50 percent minimum-tender condition and remain open for a minimum of 105 days.[11] The 50 percent tender condition means that a bid succeeds only if a majority of independent shareholders tender their securities in response to the bidder's offer. Securities of the bidder and its joint actors are not counted in the 50 percent. Once the condition is met, the new rules allow an additional ten days for undecided shareholders to tender. The majority approval requirement effectively implements collective shareholder decision-making and is akin to a shareholder vote. The reforms manifest SCG by allowing the owners of corporations to protect their own interests and thus reduce the agency costs.

Section 6.2 analyzes the role of directors' corporate-law duties in protecting shareholders' interests in changes of control and compares Canadian law and US law, which adopt different approaches in this area. Section 6.3 examines the function and purpose of the poison-pill defense, as well as the issues it creates from an SCG perspective. Section 6.4 considers the role that securities regulation plays in protecting the interests of target shareholders, particularly as a response to Canadian law's lack of a directorial duty to maximize shareholder value. It then analyzes the recently amended regime for takeovers, contending that the 50 percent tender requirement is an advance, while the 105-day bid period is misguided. Section 6.5 concludes.

6.2. Directors' Duties

In order to understand governance in the context of takeover bids, it is necessary to examine the duties of directors under corporate law. Directors' basic statutory obligation takes the form of a fiduciary duty, which applies to boards of both public and private corporations and requires directors to act honestly and in good faith with a view to the best interests of the corporation. This fiduciary duty as it appears in Canadian law also requires that directors exercise the care, diligence, and skill that a reasonably prudent person would exercise in comparable circumstances.[12] Directors' duties are consistent across provincial corporate statutes in Canada. In Delaware, the two components of directors' fiduciary duty are the duties of care and loyalty.[13] Canadian and American case law on directors' duties makes clear that the decision to adopt a poison pill or some other defensive tactic must be made in accordance with the board's fiduciary duty.[14] Where shareholders have approved the pill prior to a bid being launched, courts are unlikely to raise questions about directors' fiduciary duties.

Canadian case law has indicated that where the pill is "tactical" (i.e., adopted without shareholder approval), the target board will be protected in its decision-making by the business-judgment rule, which calls for deference to the board provided the board has weighed the risks and rewards prudently and on a reasonably informed basis.[15] According to the Canadian version of this rule, courts will look to see that the decision was made within a "range of reasonableness."[16] The target board's process in adopting the defensive tactic will be crucial and perhaps determinative of this question. Did the board consider a range of options? Did the board open its data room to other potential bidders? What considerations did the board take into account in evaluating the long-term best interests of the corporation? As the court stated in *BCE*, on any particular issue, a board's decision must be reasonable, but it is not required to be perfect.[17]

The Canadian duty must be read in light of the recent *BCE* decision, in which the Supreme Court of Canada specified that the duty is owed to the corporation rather than to a particular stakeholder group within the corporation.[18] This was a departure from American corporate law, according to which directors' duty requires them to maximize shareholder value in a change of control.[19] The Court in *BCE* explained that in any given instance, which would include a takeover bid, the board must have regard to "all relevant considerations," including "the need to treat affected stakeholders in a fair manner, commensurate with the corporation's duties as a responsible corporate citizen."[20] While the Court did not define the term *stakeholders*, it is clear that the term includes (but is not limited to) shareholders.[21]

The *BCE* case is broad and contains some ambiguity regarding the question of to whom directors owe their fiduciary duty. Commentators have called the *BCE* decision vague[22] and indeterminate.[23] What does it mean for directors to owe a duty to the nebulous and intangible thing called a "corporation"?[24] As a legal fiction, the concept of the corporation has no meaning apart from the individuals who constitute it. A duty owed to all stakeholders is diffuse indeed. Ultimately, the *BCE* decision provides boards with little clarity regarding the direction in which their duties point, instead simply reiterating the wording of the corporate statute.[25]

The United States, and particularly Delaware, generally affords more deference to directors under that state's version of the BJR. Whereas the Canadian BJR is simply an added layer of deference accorded to boards, Delaware's rule shifts the onus onto the plaintiff shareholders to prove breach once the board has been found to have acted in good faith.[26] In its usual application, this rule protects directors and officers from liability as long as the impugned transaction is made in good faith and with reasonable skill and prudence, thus providing boards with a great deal of flexibility in responding to a takeover bid.[27] However, the difference between the two interpretations of the BJR is less pronounced in changes of control, in which Delaware courts use the "enhanced scrutiny" standard, which is similar to the Canadian approach and requires courts to look critically at the process, the information relied on, and the reasonableness of the final decision.[28] Boards thus receive less latitude in the takeover context than they otherwise enjoy under Delaware corporate law.

Under Delaware law, if a court determines that a board of directors acted in good faith and in accordance with its fiduciary duties, the board is legally entitled to preserve the long-term strategic goals of the corporation. This is true even if a majority of shareholders favors an alternative approach.[29] Once it becomes apparent that the target company will be sold or broken up, however, the board's duty shifts to maximizing shareholder value, either by negotiating for improved bid terms or by seeking out and proposing an alternative transaction.[30]

US boards are unlike Canadian boards in that they are entitled to just say no to a proposed bid and to use defensive tactics, such as poison pills, to prevent, as opposed to simply delay, a bid.[31] Courts in the United States have typically held that target directors have properly satisfied their fiduciary duties when they are not acting in their own self-interest, they have reasonable grounds for believing that a particular threat to the corporation exists, they adopt reasonable measures to address the threat posed, and they act diligently on the basis of independent expert advice and full and complete information.[32] By contrast, boards in Canada have not been permitted to just say no.[33]

In the United States, the rights of target shareholders are primarily a matter of corporate law, covered by the directorial duty to maximize share value. As a consequence of this more robust corporate-law duty, securities law is not a central component of shareholder protection when it comes to takeovers and defensive tactics. Canada and the United States differ in this regard. *BCE* allows—perhaps forces—us to conclude that under Canadian corporate law, directors do not owe a duty simply to shareholders qua shareholders.[34] In departing from the American principle that boards have a duty to maximize shareholder value, Canadian law here encountered a problem that does not exist in the American context. An inconsistency emerged between corporate and securities law, as boards are able to protect interests that may not be consistent with those of the shareholders. This holding conflicts with the legislative mandate of securities regulation, discussed in previous chapters, which compels securities commissions to protect investors and maintain market efficiency.[35] The far-reaching category of "investors," which refers to shareholders in a given corporation, also includes anyone else who invests in the capital markets more broadly. A conspicuous tension arises because corporate law states that directors must take into account the interests of many stakeholders in the corporation, while securities regulation suggests that they must focus on investor (and shareholder) interests specifically.[36]

6.3. Poison Pills and Shareholder Disempowerment

When a corporation uses the poison-pill tactic to shield itself against a hostile or unwelcome takeover bid, its goal is to make the takeover more difficult and therefore less appealing to the bidder.[37] Usually, the board accomplishes this by allowing its current shareholders, not including the bidder, to purchase new shares at a discount, thus diluting the shares that the bidder has set out to acquire. In theory, this prevents hostile bidders from encouraging target shareholders to tender to an unreasonably low bid, thus making a takeover more expensive.[38]

Once the pill has been proposed, it is up to shareholders to ratify the tactic. The target corporation may put a poison-pill provision in place before any bid is launched, simply as a precautionary measure. Alternatively, a company may do so in response to a specific bid, something called a tactical pill. If the pill is ratified, the decision rests with the board to trigger it or not. In reality, this rarely happens, as the hostile bidder typically attempts to negotiate with the target or launches a proxy contest to replace the target board altogether.

The original purpose for poison pills was to stop hostile takeovers by making them prohibitively costly for the bidder.[39] As discussed above, however, Canadian law has parted from American law in permitting the use of such defensive tactics, not to halt a takeover completely but as means of granting the board the flexibility to respond to the bid. The pill allows management and the board to bargain on behalf of shareholders, to seek out a higher or more attractive offer so that shareholders do not fall prey to the tactics of the hostile bidder.[40] Without a pill, a bidder could exploit coordination problems among widely dispersed shareholders and pay less for control than if the target were to face an auction.

Poison pills are a controversial governance technique for a number of reasons. To begin with, by offering a discount to all shareholders except the bidder, the pill explicitly discriminates as between the bidder qua shareholder and all other shareholders of the target. This discrimination runs contrary to the principle of equal treatment in securities regulation that is embodied in provisions such as the identical consideration provision, which ensures that all shareholders receive the same consideration for their shares.[41]

Perhaps the greatest problem with the pill, particularly from the standpoint of SCG, is that it places a wedge between the bidder and the target shareholders to whom it has made the offer. When a pill takes effect, it puts management and the board, rather than shareholders, in the driver's seat by increasing the cost of the bid and forcing the bidder to negotiate with the board as opposed to the shareholders.

As discussed in the previous chapters, conflicts of interest can arise whenever managers have the opportunity to entrench themselves and shareholders lose control of the companies they own. The well-documented phenomenon of managerial entrenchment is a central concern of this book; SCG is largely a response to cost-creating abuses of control. As Weisbach explains: "Managerial entrenchment occurs when managers gain so much power that they are able to use the firm to further their own interests rather than the interests of shareholders."[42] The rational, self-interested actors who occupy this role may in fact act in their own best interests rather than in the corporation's, regardless of their ongoing fiduciary duty.[43]

Thus, taking bargaining power away from the shareholders and handing it over to the board and management gives rise to the concern that these agents may have conflicted loyalties.[44] In the face of a hostile takeover bid where they may lose their positions following a change of control, management and the board may make efforts to perpetuate themselves in their respective offices.[45] They may simply seek to retain their current positions or even to "extract higher wages and larger perquisites from shareholders, and obtain more latitude in determining corporate strategy."[46]

This concern with management entrenchment was the historical rationale for takeover-bid law in Canada, which sought to ensure that target shareholders were protected in change-of-control transactions,[47] which also is an important concern in the development of American law.[48] Yet some question the validity of the management entrenchment hypothesis. First, it is based on an agency cost analysis that cannot be proven definitively; one cannot determine with certainty that directors and management may seek to entrench themselves in any given situation. Second, the theory ignores the fact that senior managers and directors attempt to fulfill their fiduciary duties to the corporation, as has been recognized by the Ontario Securities Commission. According to the OSC, a measure of deference should therefore be accorded to board decisions.[49]

Of course, it is impossible to know with certainty how likely it is that boards will pursue interests at odds with the corporation's; when faced with a hostile bid, some directors may indeed seek to entrench themselves, while others will remain unconflicted. However, it is important to note that the question is not simply whether managers and the board *will* put their own interests ahead of the corporation and its stakeholders but rather whether they *may* do so. As long as management and the board have the *opportunity* to prioritize their own interests above the corporation's, the threat of management entrenchment warrants regulatory attention.

Some will argue that we should be careful to avoid becoming excessively concerned about managerial entrenchment, as such fear could lead to senior management and the board's being stripped of any or all of their powers, which would inevitably disrupt the ordinary course of business. However, the reality is that takeover contests are not the ordinary course of business. On the contrary, they disrupt the ordinary course, sometimes permanently. When an imminent takeover causes directors and senior managers to contemplate a potential loss of board seats and/or employment, the danger of management entrenchment may begin to build. Thus, it seems that lawmakers do well to respond to these situations by attempting to minimize the impact of potential conflicts of interest at the board and senior-management level.

Takeover-bid law is particularly challenging for policymakers because it requires such a delicate balancing of board authority and shareholder enfranchisement. The complexity of this exercise has made it difficult for corporate and securities law to know how to respond. Perhaps policy choices in this area should be determined with reference to the empirical literature. Jeffrey MacIntosh has persuasively argued that the "available evidence of the effects of poison pills, taken in its totality, is highly consistent with the managerial entrenchment hypothesis."[50] The evidence would therefore suggest that shareholders should be provided with more leeway in deciding the outcome of a takeover bid. Given that the purpose of securities law is to protect the interests of target shareholders, it is therefore reasonable that target shareholders should be given the choice to accept or reject the pill and, ultimately, the bid for themselves. After all, the offer is made from the bidder to the target shareholders directly, and it is therefore not necessarily within the board's discretion to make the decision.

6.4. The Role of Securities Regulators

(a) Securities Regulation and the Need for Shareholder Protection

As discussed above, there is a distinction in Canadian corporate law between the shareholders and "the corporation" as beneficiary of directorial duties. The lesson from *BCE* is that boards in Canada, unlike in the United States, are not *obliged* to act in shareholders' best interests. They may act in the interests of other stakeholders. Canadian corporate law thus leaves a gap that becomes conspicuous in the takeover-bid context. It falls to securities law to fill this gap as part of its mandate to protect the interests of the investing public. In this sense, Canadian securities law has a more important role to play in protecting shareholders' interests than we see in

American law. As I will discuss below, recent reforms to Canadian securities law on takeover bids marked an advance in this regard, although certain flaws in the legislation continue to be problematic from an SCG point of view.

The inconsistencies between securities law and corporate law have meant that boards sometimes face considerable ambiguity in understanding their legal duties, contemplating corporate law's duty to the corporation on the one hand and securities rules designed for investor protection on the other.[51] These inconsistencies are especially conspicuous in the takeover-bid context.

In light of the discussion above, one might legitimately ask whether securities law (with its obligation to shareholders) should trump corporate law (with its duty to the corporation as a whole). The simple answer, and one that is usually given, is that the shareholders are the owners of the corporation. In this sense, they are unlike other corporate stakeholders, such as creditors and employees. Accordingly, the corporate statute treats the shareholder as the central stakeholder, as evidenced by shareholders' right to elect directors and appoint auditors. Thus, the protections that securities law affords specifically to shareholders are in fact consistent with the spirit of corporate law.

What does it mean to ensure that shareholders' interests are protected in the context of a bid? One could argue that once shareholders approve a poison pill, they have entrusted the board to defend them against a bid. This is a valid argument and obviously favors allowing poison pills, at least for a limited time period. But poison pills that have not been approved by shareholders enable incumbent management and the board to thwart a bid that shareholders may wish to succeed. It is not clear that board decision-making is the best mechanism to protect shareholders' interests in this specific context.

One might further argue that boards' fiduciary duty to the corporation provides sufficient accountability or that some shareholders are in fact apathetic, suggesting that they may simply free-ride by relying on sophisticated shareholders' decision-making.[52] Even if shareholders are not apathetic, the argument may run, they have options under the corporate statute if they ultimately disapprove of the board's decisions.[53] For example, shareholders elect directors annually. They could reelect or refuse to reelect those directors. If an election is not in the offing, then shareholders have other legislative tools stipulated in the corporate statute at their disposal. They could launch a shareholder proposal, requisition a meeting, bring an oppression remedy, or launch a derivative action.

While compelling, these arguments fail to distinguish a takeover bid from the ordinary course of a corporation's business. As a change of control, a takeover bid means that the employment and roles of management and the board are potentially at stake. By contrast, a fiduciary duty to act in the best interests of the corporation in terms of deciding whether to raise capital or change the name of the corporation, to take two examples, would not impact these individuals in such a direct and significant way. And while shareholders elect directors, it is not necessarily the case that directors will act in their interests when the corporation is faced with a change of control.

Furthermore, corporate electoral machinery often fails to meaningfully involve shareholders in the proxy process. As chapter 3 discusses, shareholders lack influence over the nomination process, which seriously limits their power to choose directors.[54] Even if shareholder voting were meaningful in a given instance, shareholders would have to wait until the next annual meeting to exercise their vote or bear the expense of a dissident proxy process, which has been a successful tactic of late for only the wealthiest of shareholders.[55] Finally, a successful oppression remedy in jurisdictions where it is available means little in terms of altering a rejected change of control, especially if the bidder's offer has long expired. Courts may grant compensation to an aggrieved shareholder, but they will likely not reverse a board's decision to forgo a takeover bid.[56] If boards are permitted to keep poison pills in place indefinitely, shareholder interests may be protected, but this is far from guaranteed. Rather, shareholders' fates are subject to the discretion of the board, which, as discussed above, may or may not act in their interests.[57]

Perhaps the central argument of this book is that meaningful shareholder protection necessitates greater shareholder empowerment. Only when shareholders are able to play an active role in governance can we say that their interests are truly protected. This principle has special relevance to changes of control and should be central to any regulation in this area. Moreover, the principle of shareholder decisional authority is particularly important under corporate regimes that do not require directors to maximize value on shareholders' behalf. Next, we will examine a reform that, though imperfect, marks a significant advance toward a genuinely SCG approach to regulating takeover bids.

(b) CSA Reforms

Recent reforms to Canadian takeover law demonstrate the emergence of SCG and, indeed, the role that securities regulators can play in balancing board authority with shareholder interests in the context of defensive tactics. Prior to these reforms, there was a serious problem of uncertainty in this area of law. Rather than following clear takeover rules, securities regulators issued cease-trade orders under their amorphous public interest power, which requires no black-letter violation of securities legislation.[58] In some cases, securities commissions would accede to the board's discretion in this area, while in others, they would intervene, often providing reasons that were inconsistent with previous decisions.[59] This unpredictable, highly discretionary approach proved ineffective as a means of protecting the public interest. Shareholders, target boards, and bidders faced considerable legal uncertainty regarding the likely outcome of a given transaction.

The 2015 CSA proposal, adopted as law with very little change a year later, sought to address the problem of uncertainty while striking the difficult balance between the interests of target shareholders and those of the target board.[60] Dubbed 50-10-105, the new rules make bids subject to a mandatory (i.e., unwaivable) minimum tender condition of more than 50 percent of all outstanding target securities, excluding those held by the bidder and its joint actors. Shareholders also have an additional ten days to submit their shares after the minimum 50 percent voting-support requirement is met in order to ensure that everyone has an opportunity to respond and to prevent those who did not tender from being left as minority shareholders with no opportunity to sell later.[61] Bids can therefore only succeed with the support of a majority of independent shareholders. In essence, the bidder must obtain a majority of minority approval before it can take up shares.

The 50 percent minimum-tender condition is consistent with the central arguments of this book, weighing in favor of shareholder decision-making. The underlying rationale is that in a hostile bid, "each shareholder must ultimately be given access to an offer and the opportunity to tender."[62] Akin to a shareholder vote, this approach allows a majority of shareholders the ability to determine whether the takeover bid will succeed. Minority shareholders who wish to tender but do not because their views deviate from the majority will not have their shares taken up pursuant to the bid. In an era when shareholders are increasingly sophisticated,[63] it makes sense to allow bidders to "speak to" target shareholders directly, especially in the case of poison pills that are not approved by shareholders.

To be sure, the board continues to have a role in this process, suggesting that SCG is a phenomenon that documents the growth of shareholder power but not the replacement for board decision-making. The board prepares and distributes a directors' circular, evaluates the bid, and makes a recommendation to shareholders, which the latter can choose to follow or ignore.[64] In this instance, the directors' role gravitates toward being advisory in nature, rather than one that involves making final decisions on behalf of the shareholders. This approach has a similar result to what we see in US corporate law, which holds that the directors' role in a takeover bid shifts from that of stewards of the company to the requirement to achieve the highest price for shareholders.[65] Shareholders' interests thus trump all other concerns when the board discharges its duties. In Canada, under 50-10-105, shareholders' interests are now also of primary importance, as they (or a majority of shareholders) decide the fate of the corporation in which they have invested.

The minimum-tender condition prevents bidders from being able to corner target shareholders into the undesirable choice of selling into an underpriced offer or being stuck with illiquid shares.[66] While this amendment is laudable, the 105-day minimum bid period found in that proposal is ill conceived. Replacing the old 35-day minimum, the initial proposal was to lengthen this period to 120 days, brought down to 105 days so as to give room for a 10-day extension within the 120-day deadline under corporate statutes.[67] The rationale for the elongated bid period is "to provide target boards with a longer, fixed period of time to consider and respond to a take-over bid."[68] During this 105-day period, hostile bidders are likely to face undue exposure as their bids remain open, allowing a white knight to come forward during this time.[69] Such a long period is also likely to make the bidder's financing more expensive and more risky; financial resources that bidders have allocated to purchase the target's shares remain in limbo (i.e., unusable) while the 105-day clock ticks.

The effect of the bid period extension is to deter bids, particularly hostile bids, from occurring, which is not optimal from an economic efficiency standpoint. As argued above, takeover bids improve returns that accrue to shareholders individually as well as the performance of the overall economy.[70] It is true that the target board can reduce the 105-day period as it might in a friendly transaction. If it does, the bid must remain open for a minimum of

35 days, and all bids would be subject to the same period.[71] But the argument here is that 35 days should be the ceiling, not the floor, in terms of the time during which the target board has to act. No sound justification exists for such a lengthy bid period, with all its negative implications for target shareholders, bidders, and takeover bids generally.

Overall, the 2016 amendments facilitated SCG as they left shareholders considerably better protected than they were under the previous law. They also brought much-needed certainty to the law relating to takeover bids. Simply by laying out specific requirements for majority approval and bid periods, these reforms overcame much of the uncertainty that plagued securities law in this area for decades, which has meant less poison-pill litigation. This advance is immensely important in itself. The law—any law—should be certain for those under it to follow. The rule of law demands no less. While this principle is independent of the defining principles of SCG, it is also an indispensable part of shareholder empowerment. If securities regulators are to be effective in protecting the interests of shareholders and ensuring certainty in the capital markets, they must also be guided by coherent and specific rules.[72]

6.5. Conclusion

Poison pills adopted without shareholder approval remove decisions about the hostile bid from shareholders, allowing them to rest with the target board. This allows for board entrenchment, the antithesis of the SCG ideal this book has advocated. Indeed, the risk of entrenchment is perhaps never stronger than during a takeover, when board members realize that they may have to cling to their jobs or be evicted. As long as agency costs in the takeover-bid context exist, shareholders should be able to decide the fate of their investment.

On the whole, the 2016 CSA reforms represent an example of SCG-oriented regulation, empowering shareholders as a means of strengthening the capital markets. The new rules provide a net benefit to shareholders, despite the troublingly long 105-day bid period, which disadvantages both target shareholders and bidders by deterring desirable bids. It is counterintuitive for takeover-bid rules to have the effect of discouraging bids and thus potentially limiting the value of the shares.

Takeover bids serve to highlight the complex interplay between corporate and securities law, which is central to this book's analysis of shareholders and their rights. Sometimes corporate law serves to protect shareholders' interests, both within and beyond the takeover context. As discussed in chapter 2, corporate law's basic function in public corporations is to establish norms for the contractual relationships between shareholders and firms. Directorial duties are one set of such norms, serving in many cases to force an alignment between the authority of directors and the interests of those who have invested in the corporation. However, this alignment is imperfect if directors' duties do not require shareholder value maximization, and it then falls to securities regulation to ensure that shareholders receive protection from board decisions that affect, but do not uphold, their interests.

7

Policy Choices and Conclusions

This book represents a first step toward understanding the changing role of shareholders in the corporation. Yet one of the pressing issues not yet addressed in our discussion of SCG is the relationship of shareholders inter se. As shareholder activism influences corporate decision-making more and more, the question of whether institutional shareholders should owe fiduciary duties to other shareholders is increasingly important for corporate law. The law is certain that directors and senior managers owe a duty of loyalty to the corporation but remains unsettled regarding duties between and among the shareholders themselves. The case for the imposition of fiduciary duties on shareholders stems from the concern that shareholder opportunism needs to be managed. Institutional investors' interests may diverge from those of other shareholders in the corporation. Advocates for the imposition of shareholder fiduciary duties argue that such a change would prevent shareholder opportunism, which has the potential to harm other shareholders and the corporation.

While SCG recognizes shareholders' increasing influence in the corporation, it does not necessitate the creation of new legal duties among shareholders. Important in the analysis is a recognition of the influence of norms and their disciplining effect on large institutional shareholders, which in turn mitigate against a need for shareholder fiduciary duties.

As Licht highlights, laws are often only effective when underlying social norms encourage compliance with those laws.[1] In certain circumstances, laws can encourage the development of social norms, but absent social norms that place value on subscribing to

Shareholder-Driven Corporate Governance. Anita Indira Anand, Oxford University Press (2020).

DOI: 10.1093/oso/9780190096533.001.0001

those laws, the laws are ineffective.[2] Insofar as norms already encourage desirable behavior in the absence of laws, we can question why additional laws are needed, especially in situations where imposing new legal duties may chill the market and impose more costs than benefits (notwithstanding the difficulty in undertaking such an analysis).

Activist shareholders routinely act in ways that benefit the corporation as a whole and create positive externalities for minority shareholders. There is little evidence of systemic abuse or a pressing need for legal reform to discipline shareholders today; rather, empirical evidence demonstrates that activism can be beneficial in terms of enhancing firm value.[3] When considering whether to disrupt the status quo by imposing a shareholder fiduciary duty, regulators should be cautious about altering the current legal equilibrium.

SCG is a trend to be observed, but it is also an ideal to be achieved. Achieving this ideal calls for greater shareholder participation in corporate governance, a weighty objective that can be reached by providing shareholders with the ability to nominate directors, imposing protections in dual-class share companies, and imposing restrictions on executive compensation, for example. But SCG does not call for the amendment of a board's legal duties per se. While the Berle and Means model is no longer the prevailing paradigm with which to analyze public corporations, boards with broad-based fiduciary duties are important in order to allow SCG to take shape and in order for the corporation to flourish. As shareholder activism grows, so does the need to push our thinking about the public corporation, including a consideration and acknowledgment of SCG.

In addition to reconceptualizing our thinking about the public corporation, this book has argued that previous theories are outdated primarily because they do not consider the dominance of securities regulation in the life of a public corporation. Securities regulation has as its fundamental purpose the protection of investors. In theory, then, securities regulators will always be concerned with the concepts at the heart of SCG. Now, one may argue that sophisticated investors do not require securities regulatory oversight. But in protecting all investors, securities regulators play an important role in ensuring equal protection among investors and in maintaining efficient capital markets. This is an important mandate, to be sure, and is necessary for the benefit of all market participants.

Notes

Preface

1. Adolf Berle & Gardiner Means, *The Modern Corporation and Private Property* (revised ed. 1991).
2. Frank Easterbrook & Daniel Fischel, *The Economic Structure of Corporate Law* (1996).
3. Michael C. Jensen & William H. Meckling, *Theory of the Firm: Managerial Behavior, Agency Costs and Ownership Structure*, 3:4 J Fin Econ 305 (1976).
4. Securities legislation in Ontario already requires an analysis of the anticipated costs and benefits of a proposed rule. See Ontario Securities Act, RSO 1990, c S 5, s 143.
5. See literature on the Sarbanes-Oxley Act, including William W. Bratton, *Enron, Sarbanes-Oxley and Accounting: Rules versus Principles versus Rents*, 48:4 Villanova L Rev 1023 (2003); Kathleen F. Brickey, *From Enron to WorldCom and Beyond: Life and Crime after Sarbanes-Oxley*, 81:2 Wash Univ L Q 357 (2003); Kelly E. Carter, *Capital Structure, Earnings Management, and Sarbanes-Oxley: Evidence from Canadian and U.S. Firms*, 27:2 Accounting Horizons 301 (2013), https://papers.ssrn.com/sol3/papers.cfm?abstract_id=1664204; Teodora Paligorova, *The Effect of the Sarbanes-Oxley Act on CEO Pay for Luck*, Working Paper, Bank of Canada (2008), https://www.bankofcanada.ca/2008/06/working-paper-2008-20/; and Larry E. Ribstein, *Market vs. Regulatory Responses to Corporate Fraud: A Critique of the Sarbanes-Oxley Act of 2002*, 28:1 J Corp Law 1 (2002).
6. Stephen Bainbridge, *Corporate Governance after the Financial Crisis* (2016).
7. R. Edward Freeman & John McVea, *A Stakeholder Approach to Strategic Management* (Darden Business School Working Paper No. 01-02, 2001), https://papers.ssrn.com/sol3/papers.cfm?abstract_id=263511.
8. Lawrence E. Mitchell, *Groundwork of the Metaphysics of Corporate Law*, 50:4 Wash & Lee L Rev 1477 (1993).

9. Anita Anand et al., *Voluntary vs. Mandatory Corporate Governance Regulation: Theory and Evidence*, 14:1 Am L & Econ Rev 68 (2012).
10. Henry Hansmann & Reinier Kraakman, *The End of History for Corporate Law*, 89 Geo LJ 439 (2001), https://papers.ssrn.com/sol3/papers.cfm?abstract_id=204528.
11. See, for example, Stephen M. Bainbridge, *Director Primacy and Shareholder Disempowerment*, 119 Harv L Rev (2006); and Anita Anand & Edward Iacobucci, *The Boundaries of Corporate Law and Trust Law: An Analysis of Locking v. Mccowan*, 62:2 McGill LJ 577 (2016).
12. Jensen & Meckling, *supra* note 3.
13. *Id.*
14. Zohar Goshen & Richard Squire, *Principal Costs: A New Theory for Corporate Law and Governance*, 117:3 Colum L Rev 767 (2017).
15. See A. O. Hirschman, *Exit, Voice, and Loyalty: Responses to Decline in Firms, Organizations, and States* (1970); and Alex Edmans, *Blockholders and Corporate Governance*, 6:23 Ann Rev Fin Econ 50 (2014), http://papers.ssrn.com/sol3/papers.cfm?abstract_id=2285781.

Chapter 1

1. Berle & Means, *supra* preface note 1 at 4–6.
2. *Id.* at 9.
3. *Id.* at 7.
4. *Id.* at 18–47.
5. *Id.* at 47, 53–64. The challenges associated with this division were observed early on, as the increasing prevalence of this division between ownership and control by the mid-century led to "intense debate" over the potential deleterious effect of such separation, and whether a regulatory response was required. For more on this point, see Brian R. Cheffins, *The Public Company Transformed* (2018).
6. Wolf-Georg Ringe, *The Deconstruction of Equity: Activist Shareholders, Decoupled Risk, and Corporate Governance* 7–10 (2016).
7. The Berle and Means paradigm was not without controversy. In particular, some scholars argued that shareholders are not the "owners" of the corporation per se but rather that they hold contractual rights as a result of the share purchase without owning the corporation outright; see Lynn Stout, *The Shareholder Value Myth* (2012). We will return to this argument shortly. For an argument rejecting the idea of shareholder ownership from a different perspective, see Stephen M. Bainbridge, *Director*

Primacy: The Means and Ends of Corporate Governance 23 (UCLA School of Law Research paper no. 02-06, 2002): "In contrast, contractarians reject the idea that the firm is a thing capable of being owned. Recall that the firm is—or has—a nexus for the set of contracts by which various factors of production are hired. Someone owns each of those factors, but no one owns the nexus itself. To be sure, shareholders own the residual claim on the corporation's assets and earnings. At bottom, the ownership of that claim is why the set of contracts making up the corporation treats the shareholders as the beneficiaries of director accountability. Yet, ownership of the residual claim is not the same as ownership of the firm itself."

8. Lisa M. Fairfax, *Shareholder Democracy* 45–46 (2011).
9. See Marcel Kahan & Edward B. Rock, "Hedge Funds in Corporate Governance and Corporate Control," in William W. Bratton & Joseph A. McCahery, eds., *Institutional Investor Activism* 151 (2015). See also John Armour & Brian Cheffins, "The Rise and Fall (?) of Shareholder Activism by Hedge Funds," in William W. Bratton & Joseph A. McCahery, eds., *Institutional Investor Activism* 206 (2015).
10. Ronald J. Gilson & Jeffrey N. Gordon, *The Agency Costs of Agency Capitalism* 113:4 Colum L Rev (2011), http://columbialawreview.org/content/the-agency-costs-of-agency-capitalism-activist-investors-and-the-revaluation-of-governance-rights.
11. Brian R. Cheffins & John Armour, *The Past, Present, and Future of Shareholder Activism by Hedge Funds* 37 J of Corp L 51, 58 (2011); Armour & Cheffins, *supra* note 9.
12. Berle and Means, *supra* preface note 1 at 4–6.
13. *Id.*
14. *Report of the Attorney-General's Committee on Securities Legislation in Ontario* [*Kimber Report*] (1965). See also Stuart L. Gillan & Laura T. Starks, "The Evolution of Shareholder Activism in the United States in Institutional Investor Activism," in William W. Bratton & Joseph A. McCahery, eds., *Institutional Investor Activism* 39 (2015); Armour & Cheffins, *supra* note 9.
15. Berle & Means, *supra* preface note 1. See Gilson & Gordon, *supra* note 24. See also Lynn A. Stout, *On the Rise of Shareholder Primacy, Signs of Its Fall, and the Return of Managerialism*, 36:2 Seattle U L Rev 1169 (2013), http://digitalcommons.law.seattleu.edu/cgi/viewcontent.cgi?article=2166&context=sulr, who states, "Shareholders now have more influence over boards, and executives now are more focused on share price, than at any time in business history."

16. In addition to Stephen M. Bainbridge, *The New Corporate Governance in Theory and Practice* (2008), and *Community and Statism: A Conservative Contractarian Critique of Progressive Corporate Law Scholarship* 82:4 Cornell L Rev 856 (1997), see also Margaret M. Blair & Lynn A. Stout, *A Team Production Theory of Corporate Law*, 85:2 Va L Rev 247 (1999), https://www.business.illinois.edu/josephm/BA549_Fall%202018/Session%204/4_Blair_Stout%20(1999).pdf. Blair and Stout agree with Bainbridge's central thesis that corporate control is in the hands of directors. However, they view the role of the board differently, arguing that the board of directors acts as a "mediating hierarchy" between various interests in the corporation, such as those of the employees and shareholders. Blair and Stout's work also differs from traditional stakeholder models, since Blair and Stout believe that the current legal regime allows directors to take various interests into account, whereas "stakeholderists" believe that directors currently do not have the power to properly take into account the interests of nonshareholder constituencies.
17. Bainbridge, *The New Corporate Governance* at 5, 10–14, 19–20.
18. *Id.* at 163–187.
19. *Id.* at 35–36, 66–72. Bainbridge argues that director primacy and shareholder wealth-maximization norms are compatible for three reasons. First, shareholders will invest more when they know that these are the operationalizing norms, thus lowering a business's cost of capital and increasing their access to resources. Second, the norms hold directors accountable. By outlining a clear standard for measuring director success, directors will not be able to shirk their responsibilities. Finally, shareholders deserve this large residual right because they are the ones most at risk if managerial misconduct occurs. Unlike employees or debenture holders, shareholders are poorly positioned to extract contractual protections, since they have indefinite relationships that are rarely subject to renegotiations. See also William W. Bratton & Michael L. Wachter, "The Case against Shareholder Empowerment," in William W. Bratton & Joseph A. McCahery, eds., *Institutional Investor Activism* 769 (2015).
20. The BJR is used in both Canada and the United States. Canadian courts have been influenced by Delaware case law in their application of the BJR: *Peoples Department Stores Inc. (Trustee of) v. Wise*, 2004 SCC 68, ¶ 64. However, Delaware courts are more deferential to boards, considering only the board's process in reaching a decision, unless the transaction in question is a change of control. In such cases, they apply the "enhanced scrutiny standard," which requires review of process,

information relied on, and reasonableness of the final decision: *Unocal Corp. v. Mesa Petroleum*, 493 A2d 946 (Del 1985). In Canada, courts always apply a standard similar to "enhanced scrutiny," reviewing both the decision-making process and the reasonableness of the final decision: P. M. Vasudev, *Corporate Stakeholders in Canada—An Overview and a Proposal* 45:1 Ottawa L Rev 135, 156–158 (2012–2013). See also Nikolas Sopow, *Directors and Standards: The Problem of Insufficient Guidance* 23–29 (Electronic Thesis and Dissertation Repository 4073, 2016), https://ir.lib.uwo.ca/etd/4073.

21. Bainbridge, *The New Corporate Governance supra* note 16 at 82–88.
22. *Id.*
23. *Id.* at 27, 37–48.
24. *Id.* at 101–104, 235. Bainbridge also finishes his book with a rather remarkable statement in favor of discretion, arguing that "in sum, given the significant virtues of discretion, one ought not lightly interfere with management or the board's decision-making authority in the name of accountability. Indeed, the claim should be put even more strongly: *preservation of managerial discretion should always be [the] default presumption*"; emphasis added. Such a strong statement in favor of discretionary power in the hands of a few individuals necessarily begs the question, who monitors the monitors? Bainbridge's response is that the boards will self-monitor due to social norms and group pressures that encourage honesty and accountability. While groups may indeed be less susceptible to entrenchment when juxtaposed with imperial CEOs, a vague notion of "social pressure" is not sufficient to protect investors. Moreover, even if we assume that directors always act in the best interest of shareholders, they may simply be wrong or incompetent. For example, what if directors are taking the company in the wrong direction and shareholders wish to act before their shares have lost significant value? Bainbridge's model would make it difficult for investors to get involved in the day-to-day management of the corporation. Instead, shareholders would generally have to sit idly by as the company's share prices dropped due to director incompetence before they could exercise their limited accountability power through extreme measures such as a takeover. To expect shareholders to lose large sums of money before exercising any significant influence over the board of directors does not strike an adequate balance between accountability and authority.
25. These rights vary considerably from one jurisdiction to the next. For Canada, see Canada Business Corporations Act [CBCA], RSC 1985,

c C-44, ss 137, 143, and 239. For the American context, see Securities Exchange Act, 17 CFR § 240.14a-8 (1934) for shareholder proposals. Unlike Canada, there is no shareholder right to requisition a meeting under Delaware or US federal law. UK law does more to facilitate shareholder control, giving shareholders with 5 percent or more of a corporation a right to have their proposals included in proxy materials and to requisition meetings: Companies Act 2006 (UK), c 46, s 292. UK law does not give boards discretionary power to set aside binding proposals. I discuss the differences between shareholder rights in Canada, the United States, and the United Kingdom in chapter 3.

26. In Canada, a recent bill amended the CBCA with some provisions that enhanced shareholder democracy. Given Royal Assent on May 1, 2018, Bill C-25 requires that directors receive a majority vote and allows shareholders to vote against a nominee's election rather than simply withholding a vote. A director who receives less than a majority of votes will be removed from the board within ninety days. The bill also replaces slate voting with individual elections for individual nominees: Bill C-25, An Act to Amend the Canada Business Corporations Act, the Canada Cooperatives Act, the Canada Not-for-Profit Corporations Act and the Competition Act, 1st Sess, 42nd Parl, 2018. See also Lucian A. Bebchuk, "The Myth of Shareholder Franchise," in William W. Bratton & Joseph A. McCahery, eds., *Institutional Investor Activism* 72 (2015).
27. Anand et al., *supra* preface note 9.
28. Marianne Bradford & Joe Brazel, *Flirting with SOX 404: Are Private Companies Interested in a Relationship?* 89:3 Strat Fin 48 (2007).
29. The Public Company Accounting Reform and Investor Protection Act (Sarbanes-Oxley Act of 2002 or, SOX), 18 USC ss 1514A(a) (2002).
30. See Anand et al., *supra* preface note 9. However, the passage of SOX may indeed have resulted in greater attention being drawn to the issue of corporate disclosure undertaken by corporations. See Lawrence A. Gordon et al., *The Impact of the Sarbanes-Oxley Act on the Corporate Disclosures of Information Security Activities* 25:5 J Acc & Pub Pol'y (2006).
31. Anand et al.,*supra* preface note 9.
32. *Id.*, citing Mark Hallman, *Canadian National Railway Company—Cdn National Voluntarily Certifies Financial Reports*, Canada Stockwatch (2002); Monica Gutschi, *SEC Certification Rules Meet Little Resistance in Canada*, Dow Jones News Service (2002); *Magna Intl CEO and Fincl Chief Certify Fincl Statements*, Dow Jones News Service (2002).
33. *Id.*

34. See Peter Cziriki et al., "Shareholder Activism Through Proxy Proposals: The European Perspective," in William W. Bratton & Joseph A. McCahery, eds., *Institutional Investor Activism* 105 (2015).
35. Dodd-Frank Wall Street Reform and Consumer Protection Act, Pub L No 111-203, 124 Stat 1376 (2010).
36. Joseph E. Bachelder, *The SEC Proposed Clawback Rule*, Harvard Law School Forum on Corporate Governance and Regulation (2015), https://corpgov.law.harvard.edu/2015/10/28/the-sec-proposed-clawback-rule.
37. See Lucian A. Bebchuk & Jesse M. Fried, *Pay without Performance: The Unfuliflled Promise of Executive Compensation* (2004); see also Lucian A. Bebchuk & Jesse M. Fried, *Executive Compensation as an Agency Problem* 17:3 J of Econ Perspectives 71 (2003), https://papers.ssrn.com/sol3/papers.cfm?abstract_id=364220.
38. Ben Haimowitz, *Adoption of Clawbacks Means Stronger Link between Firm Performance and CFO Pay*, CPA Practice Advisor (2018), http://www.cpapracticeadvisor.com/news/12416039/adoption-of-clawbacks-means-stronger-link-between-firm-performance-and-cfo-pay.
39. John Tuzyk & Faye Ghadiani, *Canadian Clawbacks: Increasing but Still Voluntary*, Blakes (2014), https://www.blakes.com/English/Resources/Bulletins/Pages/Details.aspx?BulletinID=1867.
40. *Id.*
41. Etienne Farvaque et al., *Corporate Disclosure: A Review of Its (Direct and Indirect) Benefits and Costs*, 128 Intl Econ 5, 13 (2011): "Increased degree of disclosure reduces information asymmetries and the volume of informed trading. So, disclosure increases liquidity, and attracts investors to the market. The market makers will therefore increase the price at which they offer the share, which leads to a fall in the cost of capital."
42. Robert E. Verrecchia, *Discretionary Disclosure*, 5 J Acc & Econ 179 (1983).
43. Melvin Eisenberg, *Corporate Law and Social Norms*, 6:1 Colum L Rev 1253, 1280 (1999), scholarship.law.berkeley.edu/facpubs/2009.
44. *Id.* at 1279–1282.
45. Andrew MacDougall & Raphaël Amram, *Increased Shareholder Activism in Canada: A Potential Warning Sign for the Upcoming Meeting Season?*, Osler, Hoskin & Harcourt LLP (2010), https://www.osler.com/en/resources/governance/2010/corporate-review-december-2010/increased-shareholder-activism-in-canada-a-potent.
46. *Canadians' Ethical Investments Soar 68% in 2 Years*, Huffington Post (2015), http://www.huffingtonpost.ca/2015/03/12/ethical-investing-canada_n_6858514.html; Carmen Valor et al., *Understanding Demand for Retail*

Socially Responsible Investments: A Survey of Individual Investors and Financial Consultants, 16:1 Corp Soc Resp and Envtl Mgmt 1 (2009); M. E. Porter & M. R. Kramer, *The Link between Competitive Advantage and Corporate Social Responsibility*, 84:12 Harv Bus Rev 78 (2006).

47. Peter Firestein, *Crisis of Character: Building Corporate Reputation in the Age of Skepticism* (2009).
48. See Brian J. Bushee et al., *Institutional Investor Preferences for Corporate Governance Mechanisms*, 26:2 J Mgmt Acc Research 123 (2014). Bushee et al. note at 126 that "Large institutions and institutions holding a large number of stocks in their portfolios are more likely to be sensitive to corporate governance mechanisms, suggesting that institutions view governance mechanisms as a means to decrease monitoring costs."
49. Joseph A. McCahery et al., *Behind the Scenes: The Corporate Governance Preferences of Institutional Investors*, 71:6 J of Fin 2905 (2016); D. Del Guercio & J. Hawkins, *The Motivation and Impact of Pension Fund Activism*, 52:3 J Fin Econ 29 (1999); OCED, *The Role of Institutional Investors in Promoting Good Corporate Governance* (2009); Jean du Plessis et al., *Principles of Contemporary Corporate Governance* 13 (2005), remarking on the heightened ability of corporations with good corporate governance practices to attract "patient capital" (i.e., pension-fund investment).
50. Christian Pieter Hoffmann, *A Good Reputation: Protection against Shareholder Activism*, 19 Corp Reputation Rev 35 (2016), citing Guercio & Hawkins, *id.*; Kahan & Rock, *supra* note 9; William W. Bratton, *Hedge Funds and Governance Targets* (ECGI Law working paper no. 80/2007, 2007); and Alon Brav et al., "Hedge Fund Activism, Corporate Governance, and Firm Performance," in William W. Bratton & Joseph A. McCahery, eds., *Institutional Investor Activism* 261 (2015).
51. D. Diamond & R. Verrecchia, *Disclosure, Liquidity, and the Cost of Capital*, 46:4 J Fin 1325 (1991).
52. D. Miller & W. Dinan, *Revolving Doors, Accountability and Transparency—Emerging Regulatory Concerns and Policy Solutions in the Financial Crisis Organisation for Economic Co-operation and Development* (2009); David Lucca et al., *The Revolving Door and Worker Flows in Banking Regulation*, 65 J Monetary Econ 17 (2014); Ross Levine, *The Governance of Financial Regulation: Reform Lessons from the Recent Crisis*, 12:1 Int Rev Fin 39 (2011); Stefano Pagliari & Kevin L. Young, "The Wall Street–Main Street Nexus in Financial Regulation: Business Coalitions Inside and Outside the Financial Sector in the Regulation of OTC Derivatives"

(2009), in Manuela Moschella & Eleni Tsingou, *Great Expectations, Slow Transformations: Incremental Change in Financial Governance* (2013).

53. See Anita Anand & Andrew Green, *Securities Settlements as Examples of Crisis-Driven Regulation*, presentation at the Université de Montreal (working paper on file with authors, 2017).

Chapter 2

1. R. H. Coase, *The Nature of the Firm*, 4:16 Economica New Series 386 (1937).
2. *Id.*
3. Jensen & Meckling, *supra* preface note 3.
4. *Id.* at 41.
5. Easterbrook & Fischel, *supra* preface note 2; Frank Easterbrook & Dan Fischel, *The Corporate Contract*, 89 Colum L Rev 1416 (1989). See also Robert M. Daines & Michael Klausner, "Economic Analysis of Corporate Law," in Lawrence E. Blume & Stephen Durlauf, eds., *The New Palgrave Dictionary of Economics* (2008).
6. Easterbrook & Fischel, *The Corporate Contract*, at 1418.
7. Marc T. Moore, *Corporate Governance in the Shadow of the State* 65 (2013).
8. Easterbrook & Fischel, *supra* preface note 2 at 15.
9. *Id.* at 20–21: the default term should be "the term that the parties would have selected with full information and costless contracting."
10. See Bernard S. Black, *Is Corporate Law Trivial? A Political and Economic Analysis*, 84:2 Northwestern U L Rev 542 (1990). Black states at 544 that "corporate law is trivial: it does not prevent companies—managers and investors together—from establishing any set of governance rules they want."
11. For the duty of care in Canada, see section 122 of the CBCA. In Delaware, the duty is not set forth so straightforwardly; see Delaware General Corporation Law, tit 8 ss. 102(b)(7), 141, 144, and 145 (2017). Directors' duties according to Delaware law are fundamentally made up of a duty of care and a duty of loyalty. While a duty of good faith has sometimes been referred to as the third in a "triad" of duties, good faith is more commonly treated as included within the duty of loyalty; *Stone v. Ritter*, 911 A2d 362, 370 (Del 2006). Strine et al. go further and argue that care and good faith are both components of the loyalty duty; Leo Strine et al., *Loyalty's Core Demand: The Defining Role of Good Faith in Corporation Law* 7

(John M. Olin Center for Law, Economics, and Business discussion paper no. 630, 2009).

12. Alan Dignam & Michael Galanis, *The Globalization of Corporate Governance* 33–34 (2009).
13. Easterbrook & Fischel, *supra* preface note 2 at 34–36.
14. Moore, *supra* note 74 at 73.
15. *Id.* at 93.
16. *Id.* at 86.
17. Easterbrook & Fischel, *supra* note 5 at 1433.
18. *Id.* at 1444.
19. John Armour et al., *The Essential Elements of Corporate Law: What Is Corporate Law?* (John M. Olin Center for Law, Economics, and Business discussion paper no. 643, 2009).
20. Lucian A. Bebchuk & Assaf Hamdani, *Optimal Defaults for Corporate Law Evolution* (National Bureau of Economic Research working paper 8703, 2002).
21. *Id.* at 1, 5.
22. Easterbrook & Fischel, *supra* preface note 2 at 15.
23. Easterbrook & Fischel, *supra* note 5 at 1420. As the argument goes, the states' interest in attracting incorporations leads them to compete with one another to find the ideal statutory governance framework. This competition may take one of two forms: in the "race to the top" account of incorporations, management has a strong incentive to incorporate in states with corporate statutes that protect investors, because investors will not purchase shares in corporations that permit management to exploit their interests; Robert Daines, *The Incorporation Choices of IPO Firms*, 77:6 NYU L Rev 1559 (2002); Lucian A. Bebchuk & Alma Cohen, *Firms' Decisions Where to Incorporate*, 46 J L & Econ 383 (2003).
24. See Roberta Romano, *Law as a Product: Some Pieces of the Incorporation Puzzle*, 1L1 J L Econ & Org 225 (1985). Delaware is a prime example of this phenomenon, with 67.86 percent of all American incorporations happening in that state between 1996 and 2000; Bebchuk & Cohen, *Forms' Decisions*. The United States may be the only jurisdiction in which a debate about the race to the top or the bottom makes sense, as many other jurisdictions do not have substantive inconsistencies between their corporate statutes. In Canada, for example, thirteen different provinces and territories and the federal government generally operate under the same or similar corporate laws; Douglas J. Cumming & Jeffrey G. MacIntosh,

The Role of Interjurisdictional Competition in Shaping Canadian Corporate Law, 20 Intl Rev L & Econ 141, 151–152 (2000).

25. Easterbrook and Fischel take into account disclosure obligations in securities regulation (Easterbrook & Fischel, *supra* note 5 at 7) but not the securities regulatory mandate per se.
26. Margaret M. Blair & Lynn A. Stout, *A Team Production Theory of Corporate Law*, 85 Va L Rev 247 (1999). As Ben-Ishai notes, this view has had "significant impact in the American context"; see Stephanie Ben-Ishai, *A Team Production Theory of Canadian Corporate Law*, 44:2 Alta L Rev 299 (2006). For instances of such "significant impact," see *Symposium: Team Production in Business Organizations*, 24 J Corp L 743 (1999) (containing eight different articles on team production theory); Eric A. Chiappinelli, *The Moral Basis of State Corporate Law Disclosure*, 49 Catholic U L Rev 697 (2000); and Mae Kuykendall, *Assessment and Evaluation: Retheorizing the Evolving Rules of Director Liability*, 8 J Law and Policy 1 (1999). Ben-Ishai points out at 302 that "Given the significant scholarly attention Team Production Theory has received in the United States, it is surprising that it has not attracted greater attention in Canada." She does, however, note that one exception to this is the debate between Robert Yalden and Jeffrey Macintosh in the 2002 Queen's Business Law Symposium; see Robert Yalden, "Competing Theories of the Corporation and Their Role in Canadian Business Law," in Anita Anand & William F. Flanagan, eds., *The Corporation in the 21st Century: Papers Presented at the 9th Queen's Annual Business Law Symposium* 1 (2003); and Jeffrey G. MacIntosh, "The End of Corporate Existence: Should Boards Act as Mediating Hierarchs? A Comment on Yalden, in Anand & Flanagan, *id.* at 37.
27. Blair & Stout, *supra* note 26 at abstract.
28. *Id.* at 276.
29. Dignam & Galanis, *supra* note 12 at 31.
30. William W. Bratton Jr., *The "Nexus of Contracts" Corporation: A Critical Appraisal*, 74 Cornell L Rev 407, 418 (1989), scholarship.law.upenn.edu/faculty_scholarship/839/?utm_source=scholarship.law.upenn.edu%2Ffaculty_scholarship%2F839&utm_medium=PDF&utm_campaign=PDFCoverPages.
31. Jensen & Meckling, *supra* preface note 3 at 308.
32. Bratton, *supra* note 30 at 418.
33. *Id.*

34. See Jensen & Meckling, *supra* preface note 3; Andrei Shleifer & Robert W. Vishny, *Large Shareholders and Corporate Control*, 94 J Political Economy 461 (1986).
35. Zohar Goshen & Richard Squire, *Principal Costs: A New Theory for Corporate Law and Governance*, 117:3 Colum L Rev 767 (2017), http://columbialawreview.org/content/principal-costs-a-new-theory-for-corporate-law-and-governance.
36. See Black's triviality hypothesis; Black, *supra* note 10 at 544.
37. For example, see *The Role of the SEC*, Investor.gov, https://investor.gov/introduction-investing/basics/role-sec, which notes that "the U.S. Securities and Exchange Commission ('SEC') has a three-part mission: (1) Protect investors; (2) Maintain fair, orderly, and efficient markets; (3) Facilitate capital formation." In the United Kingdom, the Financial Conduct Authority works to implement the Markets in Financial Instruments Directive (MiFID), which sets out an investor protection framework that aims to ensure that investment firms act in the best interest of their clients, using a number of different approaches. See further Australian Securities & Investments Commission, *What We Do*, http://asic.gov.au/about-asic/what-we-do/our-role.
38. Yair Listokin, *What Do Corporate Default Rules and Menus Do? An Empirical Analysis*, 6:2 J of Empirical Legal Studies 284 (2008), http://digitalcommons.law.yale.edu/fss_papers/558/?utm_source=digitalcommons.law.yale.edu%2Ffss_papers%2F558&utm_medium=PDF&utm_campaign=PDFCoverPages.
39. *Id.* at 294.
40. Poonam Puri, *A Rational Allocation of Responsibility between Corporate and Securities Laws in Canada*, Osgoode Hall Law School (2004), http://digitalcommons.osgoode.yorku.ca/cgi/viewcontent.cgi?article=1111&context=reports.
41. James Park, *Reassessing the Distinction between Corporate and Securities Law*, 64 UCLA L Rev 116 (2017), papers.ssrn.com/sol3/papers.cfm?abstract_id=2779261.
42. Puri, *supra* note 40 at 10.
43. *Id.* at 13.
44. *Id.* at 9–13.
45. Sean Vanderpol & Edward J. Waitzer, *Addressing the Tension between Director's Duties and Shareholder Rights—A Tale of Two Regimes*, 50:1 Osgoode Hall LJ 5, 179–180, 188–189 (2012), digitalcommons.osgoode.yorku.ca/ohlj/vol50/iss1/5/?utm_source=digitalcommons.osgoode.

yorku.ca2Fohlj%2Fvol50%2Fiss1%2F5&utm_medium=PDF&utm_campaign=PDFCoverPages.

46. See *CTC Dealer Holdings Limited/Canadian Tire Corporation, Limited*, 10 OSC Bull 509 (Can On, 1987).
47. *Id.* at 189.
48. Yalden, *supra* note 26; see also Blair & Stout, *supra* note 26.
49. See, for instance, *Donohue v. Baja Mining*, 2016 ONSC 1569, where uncertainty over the liability cap in Securities Act influenced the court's acceptance of class counsel's arguments and the resulting settlement approval.
50. See *Kerr v. Danier Leather Inc.*, 2007 SCC 44, ¶ 54: "On the broader legal proposition, however, I agree with the appellants that while forecasting is a matter of business judgment, disclosure is a matter of legal obligation. The Business Judgment Rule is a concept well-developed in the context of *business* decisions but should not be used to qualify or undermine the duty of disclosure."
51. Easterbrook & Fischel, *supra* preface note 2 at 7.
52. *Id.*
53. Cass R. Sunstein et al., *A Behavioral Approach to Law and Economics* (1998). For an example of this kind of thinking, see Edward Iacobucci, *Making Sense of Magna*, 49 Osgoode Hall LJ 237 (2011).
54. Zohar Goshen & Gideon Parchomovsky, *The Essential Role of Securities Regulation*, 55:4 Duke LJ 711 (2006). For literature arguing the opposite (i.e., that investor irrationality warrants less intervention, see Gregory La Blanc & Jeffrey J. Rachlinski, *In Praise of Investor Irrationality* (2005).
55. See Amos Tversky & Daniel Kahneman, *Judgment under Uncertainty*, 185:4157 Science 1124 (1974).
56. For further illustration of this argument in the Russian market, see Robert J. Brown, *Of Brokers, Banks and the Case for Regulatory Intervention in the Russian Securities Markets*, 32 Stan J Intl L 185 (1996).
57. Iain MacNeil & Xiao Li, *Comply or Explain: Market Discipline and Non-Compliance with the Combined Code*, 14:5 Corp Governance: Intl Rev 486, 489 (2006), onlinelibrary.wiley.com/doi/10.1111/j.1467-8683.2006.00524.x/abstract.
58. Anita Anand, *An Analysis of Enabling vs. Mandatory Corporate Governance Structures Post Sarbanes-Oxley*, 31:1 Del J Corp L 229 (2005).
59. Robert Daines & Michael Klausner, *Do IPO Charters Maximize Firm Value? Antitakeover Protection in IPOs*, 17:1 J L Econ & Org 83 (2011). For further discussion of this point, see Anita Anand, *Governance Complexities*

in Firms with Dual Class Shares, 3:3 Ann Corp Governance 184 (2018), http://dx.doi.org/10.1561/109.00000015.

60. Securities and Exchange Commission, *What We Do*, https://www.sec.gov/about/whatwedo.shtml. See also SEC Regulatory Accountability Act, HR 1062.
61. Financial Conduct Authority, https://www.fca.org.uk/about. See also Financial Conduct Authority, *About the FCA*, https://www.fca.org.UK/about/the-fca, which states, "Financial markets need to be honest, fair and effective so that consumers get a fair deal. We aim to make markets work well—for individuals, for business, large and small, and for the economy as a whole."
62. See Securities Act (Ontario), RSO 1990, c s 5, s 1.1.
63. *Committee for the Equal Treatment of Asbestos Minority Shareholders v. Ontario (Securities Commission)* [2001], 2 SCR 132 aff'g [1999] OJ No 388 (On CA).
64. *Id.* at ¶ 41: "However, the public interest jurisdiction of the OSC is not unlimited. Its precise nature and scope should be assessed by considering s. 127 in context. Two aspects of the public interest jurisdiction are of particular importance in this regard. First, it is important to keep in mind that the OSC's public interest jurisdiction is animated in part by both of the purposes of the Act described in s. 1.1, namely 'to provide protection to investors from unfair, improper or fraudulent practices' and 'to foster fair and efficient capital markets and confidence in capital markets.' Therefore, in considering an order in the public interest, it is an error to focus only on the fair treatment of investors. The effect of an intervention in the public interest on capital market efficiencies and public confidence in the capital markets should also be considered."
65. *Id.*
66. *Re Biovali Corp.* (2010), 33 OSCB 8914 at ¶ 382, 389, 2010 CarswellOnt 7449 (Ont Securities Comm).
67. *In the Matter of Sterling Centrecorp Inc. and SCI Acquisitions Inc.* (2007), 30 OSCB 68883 at ¶ 212, 2007 CarswellOnt 4675.
68. *Costello v. Ontario (Securities Commission)* [2004], OJ No. 2927, at ¶¶ 27–28, 78–81, 132 ACWS (3d) 401.
69. *Cornish v. Ontario (Securities Commission)*, 2013 ONSC 1310 at ¶ 22, 227 ACWS (3d) 276.
70. For an overview of structural differences between the OSC and other securities commissions, namely, those in the United States, the United Kingdom, Australia, and Hong Kong, see Neil Mohindra, *The Governance*

of the Ontario Securities Commission: Lessons from International Comparisons (Fraser Institute, 2002), https://www.fraserinstitute.org/sites/default/files/OntarioSecuritiesCommission.pdf.

71. Easterbrook & Fischel, *supra* preface note 2 at 276: "Fitting these mandatory rules into the contractual framework poses something of a challenge."
72. Markus K. Brunnermeier, *Deciphering the Liquidity and Credit Crunch 2007–2008*, 23:1 J Econ Perspectives 77. Brunnermeier notes that $8 trillion of US stock-market wealth was lost between October 2007 and October 2008 alone.

Chapter 3

1. Cheffins & Armour, *supra* chapter 1 note 11.
2. See Berle & Means, *supra* preface note 1.
3. *Kimber Report, supra* chapter 1 note 14.
4. Securities Act, *supra* chapter 2 note 64 at s 86; National Instrument 51-102, Continuous Disclosure Obligations, OSC NI 51-102; CBCA, *supra* chapter 1 note 25 at s 150.
5. See Bebchuk, *supra* chapter 1 note 26.
6. Berle & Means, *supra* preface note 1.
7. Jensen & Meckling, *supra* preface note 3.
8. *Id.* See also Bebchuk, *supra* chapter 1 note 26 at 73.
9. Lucian A. Bebchuk and Ehud Kamar, *Bundling and Entrenchment*, 123:7 Harv L Rev 1549 (2010); Paul Borochin & John D. Knopf, *Do Managers Seek Control and Entrenchment?* (2016), http://papers.ssrn.com/sol3/papers.cfm?abstract_id=2670918.
10. Stephen M. Bainbridge, *Director Primacy: The Means and Ends of Corporate Governance*, 97 Northwestern U L Rev 547 (2002); Alfred D. Chandler, *The Visible Hand: The Managerial Revolution in American Business* (1977).
11. F. H. I. Cassim, *The Division and Balance of Power between the Board of Directors and the Shareholders: The Removal of Directors*, 29 BFLR 151 (2012).
12. Lucian Bebchuk, *Investors Must Have Power, Not Just Figures on Pay*, Financial Times (2006).
13. Lucian Bebchuk, *The Case for Increasing Shareholder Power*, 118 Harv L Rev 833, 833 (2005); see also L. C. Backer, *Direct Shareholder Democracy: Reflections on Lucian Bebchuk*, 2 Corp Governance L Rev 375 (2006).

14. Grant Hayden & Matthew T. Bodie, *Shareholder Democracy and the Curious Turn toward Board Primacy*, 51 Wm & Mary L Rev 2071, 2076 (2010).
15. Martin Lipton & William Savitt, *The Many Myths of Lucian Bebchuk*, 93 Va L Rev 733 (2007).
16. See also William W. Bratton & Michael L. Wachter, "The Case against Shareholder Empowerment," in William W. Bratton & Joseph A. McCahery, eds., *Institutional Investor Activism* 707 (2015).
17. CBCA, *supra* chapter 1 note 25 at s 122.
18. *Id.* at ss 137, 143, 241.
19. Innovation, Science and Economic Development Canada, *The Government of Canada Introduces a Bill to Promote Corporate Transparency and Diversity* (2016), http://m.marketwired.com/press-release/government-canada-introduces-bill-promote-corporate-transparency-diversity-2162359.htm.
20. Takeover Bids and Issuer Bids, OSC NI 62-104 (2016).
21. For a comparison between shareholders' rights in Canada and the equivalent rights in Delaware and the United Kingdom, specifically in the context of shareholders' rights plans (poison pills), see generally Ontario Securities Commission, Request for Comments, Notice and Request for Comment: Proposed NI 62-105 Security Holder Rights Plans, Proposed Companion Policy 62-105CP, and Proposed Consequential Amendments (NI 62-105, 2013), www.osc.gov.on.ca/documents/en/Securities-Category6/ni_20130314_62-105_security-holder-rights-plan.pdf. In the United Kingdom, the City Code on Takeovers and Mergers places many more restrictions on target boards than would apply in Canada. The OSC noted that the UK code "prohibits a target company board from taking any action during a bid, or in anticipation of a bid, that would frustrate the take-over bid or otherwise deny shareholders the opportunity to decide on its merits, unless such action is approved by target company shareholders in the face of the bid" (*id.* at 17).
22. *Aronson v. Lewis*, 473 A2d 805, 812 (Del 1984).
23. *Smith v. Van Gorkom*, 488 A2d 858, 873 (Del 1985).
24. Bernard S. Sharfman, *The Importance of the Business Judgment Rule*, 14:1 NYU J L & Bus 21, 30 (2017).
25. *Id.* at 33.
26. *Paramount Communications Inc v. QVC Network Inc.*, 637 A2d 34 (Del. 1993), Civil Action No. 5249-CC (Del) (Ch 2011) (QL).
27. Kahan & Rock, *supra* chapter 1 note 9.

28. *Revlon Inc. v. MacAndrews & Forbes Holdings Inc.*, [1986] 506 A2d 173 (Del).
29. See Jennifer G. Hill & Matthew Conaglen, "Directors' Duties and Legal Safe Harbours: A Comparative Analysis," in D. Gordon Smith and Andrew S. Gold, eds., *Research Handbook on Fiduciary Law*, 305–330 (2018), https://papers.ssrn.com/sol3/papers.cfm?abstract_id=2942758.
30. See *In re City Equitable Fire Insurance Co.*, [1925] Ch 407.
31. S 174 of the UK Companies Act 2006, *supra* chapter 1 note 25 at c 46, requires a director to act with "the care, skill and diligence that would be exercised by a reasonably diligent person with—(a) the general knowledge, skill and experience that may reasonably be expected of a person carrying out the functions carried out by the director in relation to the company, and (b) the general knowledge, skill and experience that the director has." See also *Re D'Jan of London Ltd.*, [1993] BCC 646; *Norman v. Theodore Goddard*, [1992] BCC 14. Even with this stricter standard, UK courts remain reluctant to hold directors liable for honest mistakes; Hill & Conaglen, *supra* note 29.
32. Edmans, *supra* preface note 15; Albert O. Hirschman, *Exit, Voice and Loyalty* (1970). For a seminal theoretical paper on the role of activists in reducing agency costs, see also Andrei Shleifer & Robert W. Vishny, *Large Shareholders and Corporate Control*, 94 J of Political Economy 461 (1986).
33. Edmans, *supra* preface note 15 at 24.
34. *Id.*
35. Lucian Bebchuk, *The Law and Economics of Activist Disclosure*, 2 Harv Business L Rev 39, 47 (2012).
36. Henrik Cronqvist & Rudiger Fahlenbrach, *Large Shareholders and Corporate Policies*, 22:10 Rev Fin Stud 3941 (2009); Edmans *supra* preface note 15; Clifford G. Holderness, *A Survey of Blockholders and Corporate Control*, 9:1 Econ Policy Rev 51 (2003); Marco Becht et al., "Returns to Shareholder Activism: Evidence from a Clinical Study of the Hermes U.K. Focus Fund," in William W. Bratton & Joseph A. McCahery, eds., *Institutional Investor Activism* 223 (2015); Brav et al., *supra* chapter 1 note 50; April Klein & Emanuel Zur, "Entrepreneurial Shareholder Activism: Hedge Funds and Other Private Investors," in William W. Bratton & Joseph A. McCahery, eds., *Institutional Investor Activism* 305 (2015).
37. Bebchuk, *supra* note 35.
38. Andrew Winton, *Limitation of Liability and Ownership Structure of the Firm*, 48:2 J Fin 487 (1993).

39. *Id.*
40. Amrita Dhillon & Silvia Rossetto, *Corporate Control and Multiple Large Shareholders* (University of Warwick working paper, 2009), https://www2.warwick.ac.uk/fac/soc/economics/staff/academic/dhillon/wp/submission16nov09.pdf.
41. Winton, *supra* note 38.
42. John Armour et al., *Agency Problems, Legal Strategies and Enforcement* (Harvard John M. Olin Discussion Paper Series no. 644, 2009), http://www.law.harvard.edu/programs/olin_center/papers/pdf/Kraakman_644.pdf. Although the presence of a single large activist tends to increase shareholder monitoring of management, it is worth bearing in mind the possibility that the activist will seek to extract private benefits of control to the detriment of other shareholders.
43. Andrew Kulpa, *The Wolf in Shareholder's Clothing*, 6 UC Davis Bus LJ 4 (2005). Cheffins cites diffuse share ownership as a key factor in the rise of "managerial capitalism". See Cheffins *supra* Chapter 1 note 5.
44. Armour et al., *supra* note 42. It is worth noting, however, that the coordination issues that hinder shareholder intervention strategies actually make the threat of exit stronger, thereby allowing many small activists to have a positive impact on managerial discipline: Alex Edmans & Gustavo Manso, *Governance through Trading Intervention: A Theory of Multiple Blockholders*, 24:7 Rev Fin Stud 2395 (2010), argue that the threat of trading activity of multiple activists in the face of poor managerial performance disciplines management. Even so, wolf packs ostensibly form to intervene and agitate for change, not to passively invest and then exit.
45. For example, in 2017, 62 percent of shareholders voted against ExxonMobil management in favor of a resolution to disclose how climate change impacts business; Ed Crooks, *ExxonMobil Bows to Shareholder Pressure on Climate Reporting*, Financial Times (2017), https://www.ft.com/content/8bd1f73a-dedf-11e7-a8a4-0a1e63a52f9c. See also Gaia Balp, *The Corporate Role of Retail Investors* (Bocconi Legal Studies research paper, 2018), https://papers.ssrn.com/sol3/papers.cfm?abstract_id=3193356.
46. Bebchuk calls the short-termism argument "the strongest objection to [corporate] election reform"; Bebchuk, *supra* chapter 1 note 26. Kahan and Rock call the same argument "the sharpest and most comprehensive criticism of hedge fund activism"; Kahan & Rock, *supra* chapter 1 note 9. For empirical analysis of the short-termism phenomenon before the GFC, see Brian J. Bushee, *Do Institutional Investors Prefer Near-Term Earnings over Long Run Value?* 18:2 Contemporary Accounting Research 207 (2001),

https://papers.ssrn.com/sol3/papers.cfm?abstract_id=161739. See also Lynne L. Dallas, *Short-Termism, the Financial Crisis, and Corporate Governance* 37 J Corp L 265 (2011), https://papers.ssrn.com/sol3/papers.cfm?abstract_id=2006556.

47. For instance, Bushee, *supra* note 46, argues that the presence of significant institutional blockholders is positively correlated with concentration on short-term earnings over long-term value creation, such as through research and development.
48. Sham Gad, *What Are Hedge Funds?* Forbes (2013), www.forbes.com/sites/investopedia/2013/10/22/what-are-hedge-funds.
49. Bennelong, *Debunking Hedge Fund Myths*, Century Private Wealth (2016), www.centuryprivatewealth.com.au/news/view/debunking_hedge_fund_myths.
50. Brent Jang, *As Harrison Takes CP's Top Job, Ackman's Coup Is Complete*, Globe and Mail (2013), www.theglobeandmail.com/globe-investor/as-harrison-takes-cps-top-job-ackmans-coup-is-complete/article4379406.
51. Brent Jang, *Activist Investor Ackman Unloads $835-million CP Stake*, Globe and Mail (2013), www.theglobeandmail.com/report-on-business/ackman-unloads-835-million-cp-stake/article15065221.
52. *Id.*
53. A. J. Atkinson et al., *2013 Canadian Proxy Contest Study*, Fasken Martineau (2013), https://www.fasken.com/en/knowledge/2013/01/anextensiveempiricalstudyof-20130125//.
54. Lionsgate enacted a poison-pill provision in 2010 to discourage a shareholder's "creeping bid." After implementation, Lionsgate's share price increased from CAD$7.00 to CAD$14.80.
55. In 2012, EnerCare offered to pay brokers a solicitation fee of CAD$0.05 for each share voted by a retail shareholder in favor of board reelection. EnerCare's share price improved from CAD$9.90 in April 2012 to CAD$15.85 in April 2016.
56. Share price data from TMX Money.
57. *Id.*
58. Paul Rose & Barnard S Sharfman, *Shareholder Activism as a Corrective Mechanism in Corporate Governance*, BYU L Rev 1015 (2014). The evidence is mixed with respect to mergers and takeovers following proxy contests. There have been some cases in which shareholder activists have won (or partially won) a proxy battle, but a merger or takeover followed. For example, Biovail merged with Valeant Pharmaceuticals following a partial victory by shareholder activists. Pet Valu was also involved in a

merger following a victory by shareholders in a proxy contest. This is not to say that a merger or acquisition will always occur after a shareholder victory in a proxy contest, as the example of Hudbay Minerals demonstrates. It was not involved in an acquisition or merger.

59. Marco Becht et al., *Returns to Hedge Fund Activism: An International Study*, 30:9 Rev Fin Stud 2933 (2017), https://academic.oup.com/rfs/article/30/9/2933/3852480. This finding is based on data for activist interventions internationally from 2000 to 2010.
60. Brav et al., *supra* chapter 1 note 50. See also Lucian A. Bebchuk et al., *The Long-Term Effects of Hedge Fund Activism*, 115 Colum L Rev 1085 (2015), finding a 6 percent abnormal return for the same period relative to announcement, covering activist interventions from 1994 to 2007.
61. Andrew Carrothers, *Friends or Foes? Activist Hedge Funds and Other Institutional Investors*, 3:17 Eco & Bus Rev 38 (2017).
62. Bebchuk et al, *supra* note 60.
63. *Id.*
64. Dionysia Katelouzou, *Myths and Realities of Hedge Fund Activism: Some Empirical Evidence*, 7 Va L & Bus Rev 459, 504 (2013).
65. Ontario Teachers' Pension Plan, *Among the Most Successful in the World, the Total Value of Canada's Ten Largest Public Pension Funds Has Tripled since 2003* (2015), https://www.otpp.com/news/article/-/article/750139.
66. Guillaume Bédard-Pagé et al., *Large Canadian Public Pension Funds: A Financial System Perspective* 33 (Bank of Canada, 2016), https://www.bankofcanada.ca/wp-content/uploads/2016/06/fsr-june2016-bedard-page.pdf.
67. *Id.* at 33–34.
68. For example, prior to Bombardier's 2017 annual meeting, the company proposed that executive chair Pierre Beaudoin stand for reelection. Major pension funds including the OTPP, CDPQ, CPP, the Quebec Federation of Labour's Solidarity Fund, and British Columbia Investment Management Corporation stated their opposition and intention to vote against Beaudoin's reelection. The investors made public statements about their lack of support and are said to have voted against Beaudoin and a proposed executive compensation plan. Beaudoin ultimately gave up his management role, although he remained part of the board. See Alicja Siekierska, *Ontario Teachers' Pension Plan Withholds Support for Re-election of Bombardier's Executive Chairman*, Financial Post (2017), http://business.financialpost.com/transportation/ontario-teachers-pension-plan-votes-against-re-election-of-bombardiers-executive-chairman;

Patti Waldmier & Pan Kwan Yuk, *Bombardier Chairman Forced out of Executive Role*, Financial Times (2017), https://www.ft.com/content/b8eb3d58-3651-11e7-bce4-9023f8c0fd2e.

69. *Kimber Report, supra* chapter 1 note 14.
70. Bebchuk, *supra* chapter 1 note 26.
71. See Peter Cziraki et al., "Shareholder Activism through Proxy Proposals: The European Perspective," in William W. Bratton & Joseph A. McCahery, eds., *Institutional Investor Activism* 105 (2015).
72. CBCA, *supra* chapter 1 note 25 at s 137(4). For an example of how courts approach this rule, see *National Bank v. Weir*, 2009 QCCS 5688, in which the Quebec Superior Court granted a motion by National Bank to exclude thirty-eight proposals by a shareholder in the Management Proxy Circular under the Bank Act (SC 1991, c. 46) proposal provisions, namely, s. 143(5)(b) and (e), which are virtually identical to the proposal provisions in s. 137(5)(b) and (e) of the CBCA. The court held that although a proposal may appear to be neutral on its face, it must be read and considered in context. The court found that in light of the timing and circumstances, it was evident that the proposals by the respondent were abusive, even though in normal circumstances these "might be considered his rights as shareholder." The court also noted that there was not an abundance of case law on this subject, since the proposal mechanism was rarely used in Canada until recently.
73. *Id.* CBCA at s 150; Canada Business Corporations Regulations, SOR/2001-512, s 57. See also Canadian Coalition for Good Governance (CCGG), *Shareholder Involvement in the Director Nomination Process: Enhanced Engagement and Proxy Access* (2015), www.ccgg.ca/site/ccgg/assets/pdf/proxy_access_finalv.35.docx_630.pdf,
74. *Id.* CBCA at s 143.
75. Securities Exchange Act (SEA), 17 CFR § 240.14a-8 (1934).
76. *Id.* at 14a-8(i)(8). See also David C. Donald, *The Nomination of Directors under U.S. and German Law* 12 (Institute for Law and Finance working paper no. 21, 2004), https://www.ilf-frankfurt.de/fileadmin/_migrated/content_uploads/ILF_WP_021.pdf
77. *Id.* SEA at 14a-4(d)(1).
78. See Securities and Exchange Commission, *Recommendations of the Investor Advisory Committee Regarding SEC Rulemaking to Explore Universal Proxy Ballots* (2013), https://www.sec.gov/spotlight/investor-advisory-committee-2012/universal-proxy-recommendation-072613.pdf.

79. See Alexander Schmitt, *Why Are Activist Investors Drawn to Canada?* Special Situations Law (2014), https://www.specialsituationslaw.com/2014/05/26/why-are-activist-investors-drawn-to-canada.
80. SEA, *supra* note 75 at rule 14a-11.
81. Shifeng Ni, *Proxy Access Revisited: Regulatory Function of the Rule 14a-11 Formula*, CLS Blue Sky Blog (2015), http://clsbluesky.law.columbia.edu/2015/10/30/proxy-access-revisited-regulatory-function-of-the-rule-14a-11-formula; *Business Roundtable v. Securities and Exchange Commission*, 647 F (3d) 1144 (DC Cir 2011).
82. Securities and Exchange Commission, *Proposed Rule 34-79164, Universal Proxy* (2016), https://www.sec.gov/rules/proposed/2016/34-79164.pdf.
83. See Jill E. Fisch, "The Destructive Ambiguity of Federal Proxy Access," in William W. Bratton & Joseph A. McCahery, eds., *Institutional Investor Activism* 636 (2015).
84. Paula Loop, *The Changing Face of Shareholder Activism* (Harvard Law School Forum on Corporate Governance and Financial Regulation, 2018), https://corpgov.law.harvard.edu/2018/02/01/the-changing-face-of-shareholder-activism.
85. In the United States, this discretionary power comes from the Securities Exchange Act of 1934, 17 CFR § 240.14a-8(i)(1). See Doron Levit & Nadya Malenko, *Nonbinding Voting for Shareholder Proposals*, 66:5 J Fin 1, 2, 5 (2011), for an explanation of the effect that this provision has on proposals and of the difference between binding and nonbinding proposals. In Canada, see CBCA, *supra* chapter 1 note 25 at s 137(5), discussed above. See also Canadian Coalition for Good Governance (CCGG), *Shareholder Involvement in the Director Nomination Process: Enhanced Engagement and Proxy Access* (2015), https://www.ccgg.ca/site/ccgg/assets/pdf/proxy_access_finalv.35.docx_630.pdf.
86. Companies Act, *supra* chapter 1 note 25.
87. *Id.* at s 303.
88. *Id.* at s 160.
89. Special resolutions such as amendments to the articles of association require a supermajority of 75 percent; *id.* at ss 282, 283.
90. Vanderpol & Waitzer, *supra* chapter 2 note 45 at 177.
91. Bebchuk, *supra* chapter 1 note 13. Supporters of "management insulation" will counter this argument and assert that shareholders should not be given the right to nominate directors, since shareholder interests in the corporation are often short-term as opposed to long-term and in general are motivated by considerations other than enhancing the

corporation's long-term interests. Those concerned with the possibility of increased shareholder power may also argue that shareholder nomination power could lead to the board being "co-opted" such that it represents the interests of a particular shareholder rather than the corporation as a whole.

92. In Canada, see CBCA, *supra* chapter 1 note 25 at s 122. In the United States, see Delaware General Corporation Law (DGCL), tit 8 ss 102(b)(7), 141, 144, and 145 (2017). In the United Kingdom, see Companies Act, *supra* chapter 1 note 25 at ss 171–177.
93. CCGG, *supra* note 73.
94. This is currently the system in Italy. See CCGG *id.* for other international examples. See also David A. Skeel Jr. et al., *Inside-Out Corporate Governance*, 37 J Corp L 147 (2011), for more details on the Italian system.
95. William W. Bratton, *Hedge Fund Activism, Poison Pills and the Jurisprudence of Threat*, CLS Blue Sky Blog (2016), http://clsbluesky.law.columbia.edu/2016/10/06/hedge-fund-activism-poison-pills-and-the-jurisprudence-of-threat. Bratton makes a similar point—that the existing chasm between those for and against shareholder activism is not necessary—but advances a much different reform proposal. Bratton's idea revolves around asking the question whether a 5 percent poison pill can have policy benefits. He states, "Some [companies] are appropriate targets for activist intervention, while others are not . . . company-by-company dialogue on the point would be a good thing, exploring the possibility that a 5 percent standing pill could trigger useful informational exchanges between managers and institutional investors without simultaneously overdeterring activist intervention." See also Lucian A. Bebchuk, "The Myth of Shareholder Franchise," in William W. Bratton & Joseph A. McCahery, eds., *Institutional Investor Activism* 72 (2015), who states: "My support for reforming corporate elections is not motivated by political ideas but rather by the goal of making a market institution—the modern publicly traded company—function better. If the absence of viable shareholder power to replace directors was expected to produce better corporate performance and higher shareholder value, I would fully support a corporate governance system lacking such power. I support a viable shareholder power to replace directors only because I view it as a valuable instrument for enhancing shareholder value by making boards more accountable and more attentive to shareholder interests."
96. Michael E. Murphy, *Assuring Responsible Risk Management in Banking: The Corporate Governance Dimension*, 36 Del J Corp L 121 (2011).

97. Michael E. Murphy, *Restoring Trust in Corporate America: Toward a Republican Theory of Corporate Legitimacy*, 5 NYU J L & Bus 415 (2009).
98. *Id.*
99. Rafael La Porta et al., *Investor Protection and Corporate Governance*, 58:3 J Fin Econ 15 (2000). In the cross-border merger context, merger premiums tend to be higher in countries with better shareholder protection. On this point, see Arturo Bris and Christos Cabolis, *The Value of Investor Protection: Firm Evidence from Cross-Border Mergers*, 21:2 Rev Fin Stud 605 (2008).
100. Lucian A. Bebchuk, *The Myth That Insulating Boards Serves Long-Term Value*, 113 Colum L Rev 1637 (2013). See also Bebchuk, *supra* note 35.

Chapter 4

1. According to the *Dickerson Report*, balancing the tension between directors and shareholders is the normative underpinning of Canadian corporate law: "We cannot see any practical reason that, at least in the public corporation, shareholders should be involved with corporate administration. This is not to say, however, that directors should not be responsible for their actions and accountable to shareholders and others for what they do"; Robert Dickerson et al., *Proposal for a New Business Corporations Law for Canada* 3 (Information Canada, 1971).
2. See Berle & Means, *supra* preface note 1.
3. Balp, *supra* chapter 3 note 45. Smaller shareholders may also play an important corporate governance role in monitoring controlling shareholders.
4. John C. Coffee & Darius Palia, *The Wolf at the Door: The Impact of Hedge Fund Activism on Corporate Governance*, 1:1 Ann Corp Governance 1 (2016), http://papers.ssrn.com/sol3/papers.cfm?abstract_id=2496518; John C. Coffee, "Hedge Fund Activism: What Do We Know and Not Know?" in William W. Bratton & Joseph A. McCahery, eds., *Institutional Investor Activism* 701–705 (2015). See also Anita Anand & Andrew Mihalik, *Coordination and Monitoring in Changes of Control*, 54:2 Osgoode Hall L J 377 (2017).
5. Anand & Mihalik, *id.*
6. Brent Jang & Jacquie McNish, *CPPIB Backs Pershing Square in CP Proxy Row*, Globe and Mail (2012), http://www.theglobeandmail.

com/globe-investor/cppib-backs-pershing-square-in-cp-proxy-row/article4106482.

7. Yu Ting Forrester Wong, *Wolves at the Door: A Closer Look at Hedge Fund Activism* (Columbia Business School research paper no. 16-11, 2016), http://papers.ssrn.com/sol3/papers.cfm?abstract_id=2721413; Anita Anand, *Shareholder Activism in Proxy Contests*, Can Investment Rev (2015), http://www.investmentreview.com/files/2015/03/ProxyContests_Anita-Anand.pdf; Anita Anand, "Implications of Shareholder Activism," in P. M. Vasudev & Susan Watson, eds., *Global Capital Markets* 17 (2017).
8. Anand & Mihalik, *supra* note 5.
9. *Id.*
10. Richard Bozec et al. find that 58 percent of Canadian issuers feature at least one controlling shareholder that owns shares representing more than 10 percent of the voting rights in respect to the issuer; Richard Bozec et al., *Corporate Ownership and Governance Practices in Canada: A Longitudinal Study*, 4:1 J Intl Corp Governance 51 (2015). See also Randall K. Morck et al., "Inherited Wealth, Corporate Control and Economic Growth: The Canadian Disease?" in Randall K. Morck, ed., *Concentrated Corporate Ownership* (2000).
11. For a more detailed explanation of these hypotheses, see Wong, *supra* note 7.
12. Coffee and Palia, *supra* note 4 at 34.
13. Alon Brav et al., *Wolf Pack Activism* (Robert H. Smith School research paper no. RHS 2529230, 2016), http://papers.ssrn.com/sol3/papers.cfm?abstract_id=2529230.
14. Securities Act, *supra* chapter 2 note 64 at s 102.1. Furthermore, shareholders in US corporations have a ten-day window in which to purchase additional shares after crossing the 5 percent threshold, while shareholders in Canadian corporations must immediately cease the purchase of additional shares upon hitting the 10 percent threshold.
15. Coffee and Palia, *supra* note 4 at 34.
16. Becht et al., *supra* chapter 3 note 36.
17. Anand & Mihalik, *supra* note 4.
18. Coffee and Palia, *supra* note 4 at 34.
19. *Id.*
20. William W. Bratton, *Hedge Funds and Governance Targets: Long-Term Results* 1384 (University of Pennsylvania Institute for Law and Economics

research paper no. 10-17, 2010), http://papers.ssrn.com/sol3/papers.cfm?abstract_id=1677517.

21. In particular, each member of the wolf pack would be careful to avoid being classified as an "insider" or in a "special relationship with the reporting issuer."
22. Brav et al., *supra* chapter 3 note 36.
23. Securities Act, *supra* chapter 2 note 62 at s 102.1.
24. For instance, crossing the 10 percent ownership threshold requires the shareholder to immediately cease subsequent purchases in the issuer for a full business day and immediately file a disclosure report and will implicate insider trading and tipping laws based on the shareholder's "special relationship" with the issuer.
25. Coffee and Palia, *supra* note 4 at 34.
26. For example, Pershing Square's 2006 activist campaign in respect of Canadian Tire Corp. was halted in its tracks by the daughter of a cofounder of the company, who controlled 61 percent of the company's voting shares through a dual-class structure; Lori McLeod, *US Hedge Fund Kicks the Tire*, Financial Post (2006).
27. Bozec, *supra* note 10.
28. Walid Ben-Amar & Paul Andre, *Separation of Ownership from Control and Acquiring Firm Performance: The Case of Family Ownership in Canada*, 33:3 J Bus Fin & Accounting 517, 518 (2006).
29. Simi Kedia et al., *Institutional Investors and Hedge Fund Activism* (Rutgers working paper, 2018). Kedia et al. found that the presence of any institutional ownership increases a firm's likelihood of being targeted by a wolf pack. Where the institution is activism-friendly, the chance of being targeted is further increased.
30. For recent statistics on pension-fund ownership of Canadian equities, see Vijay Jog & Jack Mintz, *Sovereign Wealth and Pension Funds Controlling Canadian Businesses: Tax-Policy Implications*, 6:5 SPP Research Papers 1 (2013), https://www.policyschool.ca/wp-content/uploads/2016/03/jogmintz-pensionwealth.pdf.
31. John A. Doukas et al., *Security Analysis, Agency Costs and Company Characteristics*, 56:6 Fin Analysts J 54 (2000).
32. *Re Magna International Inc.* (2010), 34 OSCB 1290.
33. Becht et al., *supra* chapter 3 note 36 at 2959 (which finds a 78 percent success rate for wolf packs compared with a 46 percent success rate for other activists).
34. John C. Coffee, *Hedge Fund Activism: A Guide for the Perplexed*, CLS Blue Sky Blog (2016), http://clsbluesky.law.columbia.edu/2016/01/25/hedge-fund-activism-a-guide-for-the-perplexed.

35. In the United States, empirical studies have indicated that Schedule 13D disclosure results in a positive abnormal share price appreciation (even if only in the short term). As such, members of wolf packs in respect of US companies that purchase shares before the lead member of the pack files its disclosure obtain a riskless profit; see Coffee, *supra* note 4 at 10, and, on other empirical effects of shareholder activism, Brav et al., *supra* chapter 1 note 50. See also Bebchuk et al., *supra* chapter 3 note 60. To the extent that public knowledge of an activist involvement with an issuer would result in a similar share price appreciation in Canada with the filing of an early-warning report, members of the wolf pack have a similar opportunity at riskless profit when the lead member of the pack announces its position.
36. Empirical work has shown that the announcement of a proxy contest is associated with positive abnormal share price appreciation; Lisa F. Borstadt & Thomas J. Zwirlein, *The Efficient Monitoring Role of Proxy Contests: An Empirical Analysis of Post-Contest Control Changes and Firm Performance*, 21 Fin Mgmt 22 (1992).
37. This exemption allows a dissident shareholder to communicate with other shareholders through a website, press release, public broadcast, or public speech without having to prepare and mail a proxy circular; Continuous Disclosure Obligations, OSC NI 51-102, 36 OSCB 2619 (May 31, 2013) s 9.2.
38. *Id.* at s 9.2. This exemption contrasts with the relatively stricter shareholder communication and proxy rules in the United States. For a discussion of these rules, see Stephen Choi, *Proxy Issue Proposals: Impact of the 1992 SEC Proxy Reforms*, 16 JL Econ (2000), http://papers.ssrn.com/sol3/papers.cfm?abstract_id=219933.
39. On the efficient-markets hypothesis, see Eugene F. Fama, *Efficient Capital Markets: A Review of Theory and Empirical Work*, 25:2 J Fin 383 (1970).
40. On the relationship between disclosure and price efficiency, see Anita Anand, *Fairness at What Price? An Analysis of the Regulation of Going-Private Transactions in OSC Policy 9.1*, 43 McGill LJ 115 (1998). On the importance of price efficiency in the public markets, see Fama, *supra* note 39.
41. Paul G. Mahoney, *Mandatory Disclosure as a Solution to Agency Problems*, 62:3 U Chicago L Rev 1047, 1048 (1995). See also Lucian A. Bebchuk & Robert J. Jackson Jr., "The Law and Economics of Blockholder Disclosure," in William W. Bratton & Joseph A. McCahery, eds., *Institutional Investor Activism* 617 (2015).

42. See Wong, *supra* note 7 at 31, who states that "timely and reliable disclosures constrain the ability of blockholders to secure private benefits."
43. Coffee, *supra* note 4 at 30–32.
44. Wong, *supra* note 7 at 28–39.
45. Coffee, *supra* note 4 at 33–34; Bebchuk, *supra* chapter 3 note 100.
46. Coffee, *supra* note 4 at 33–34.
47. See Coffee, *supra* note 4 at 82.
48. Michael J. Barclay & Clifford G. Holderness, *Private Benefits from Control of Public Corporations*, 25 J Fin Econ 371 (1989).
49. *Continental Precious Metals Inc. v. Singh*, 2012 ONSC 7122 [Commercial List] at ¶ 12.
50. Securities Act, *supra* chapter 2 note 64 at s 102.1.
51. *Id.* at s 91(1).
52. See, for instance, *Re Sears Canada* (2006), 35 OSCB 8781, and *Re Sterling Centrecorp Inc.* (2007), 30 OSCB 6683. These decisions, and the others that interpret this statutory language, do so in the context of takeover bids, insider bids, and related party transactions. The OSC's decision in *Re Sterling Centrecorp* is exemplary of the fact-specific nature of these decisions and the difficulty in applying them to wolf packs: the "policy underlying the concept of identifying who is a 'joint actor' . . . is to ensure that all persons or companies that are effectively engaged in a common investment or purchase program are required to abide by the requirements of Ontario securities laws" and, further, that a "determination of a joint actor relationship can be made if the facts establish that the parties in question played an integral role in planning, promoting and structuring the transaction to ensure its success beyond their customary role." An added issue is that many decisions that address the concept of "acting jointly or in concert" do so with reference to the definition of "joint actor" under certain national and multilateral instruments relating to takeover bids. It is an open question whether decisions determining a "joint actor" characterization under takeover-bid rules would apply to the determination of whether shareholders are "acting jointly or in concert" for the purposes of early-warning reporting.
53. Securities Exchange Act of 1934, 48 Stat 881 (codified as amended at 15 USD §§ 78m(d)(1)–(7)).
54. *Id.* at §§ 78m(d)(1).
55. *Id.* at §§ 78m(g).
56. *Id.* at §§ 78p(a)(1). For example, the shareholder may have to forfeit its profits on sales of shares past the 10 percent threshold.

57. *Id.* at §§ 78m(d)(3).
58. *CSX Corp. v. Children's Inv. Fund Mgmt. (U.K.), LLP*, 562 F Supp 2d 511, 525 (S.D.N.Y. 2008) at 553.
59. *Id.* at 553.
60. Coffee, *supra* note 4 at 28.
61. US Securities and Exchange Commission, *Corporate Insiders Charged for Failing to Update Disclosures Involving "Going Private" Transactions*, press release 2015-47 (2015), https://www.sec.gov/news/pressrelease/2015-47.html#.VQ0KKeFi52A.
62. As the CSA noted, "the mere identity and presence of an institutional shareholder may be material to some investors." See Canadian Securities Administrators, Ontario Securities Commission, *CSA Notice and Request for Comment: Proposed Amendments* (2014), https://www.osc.gov.on.ca/en/SecuritiesLaw_mi_20130313_62-104_take-over-bids.htm.
63. See *Hallwood Realty Partners LP v. Gotham Partners LP*, 286 F3d 613 (2d Cir 2002); and Coffee, *supra* note 4 at 39.
64. *20099 Ontario Inc. v. Harold E Ballard Ltd.*, (1992), 3 BLR (2d) 113 (Ont SCJ), cited in *Genesis Land Development Corp. v. Smoothwater Capital Corp.*, 2013 ABQB 509 at ¶ 69.
65. *Genesis v. Smoothwater, id.* at ¶¶ 70–71.
66. Coffee, *supra* note 4 at 42.
67. *Disclosure Standards*, OSC NP 51-201, (2013) 25 OSCB 4492.
68. See Securities Act, *supra* chapter 2 note 64 at s 76(3).
69. And in any event, both would be expected to have significant impacts on the value of a given company's securities.
70. Thomas W. Briggs, *Corporate Governance and the New Hedge Fund Activism: An Empirical Analysis*, 32 J Corp L 681, 698 (2007).

Chapter 5

1. Goshen & Squire, *supra* chapter 1 note 1.
2. While the focus of this chapter is on public MVS firms, private firms can also have MVSs, as long as the structure is specified in the firm's articles of incorporation. Between 1979 and 1983, the number of MVS companies listed on the Toronto Stock Exchange (TSX) increased from 64 to 130. The current number is around 80. See Matthew Merkley, *Multiple Voting Shares: Don't Call It a Comeback*, Blake, Cassels & Graydon LLP (2015), http://www.blakes.com/English/Resources/TrendsInsights/Pages/details.aspx?AnnouncementID=78.

3. Henry Hu & Bernard Black, "Debt, Equity, and Hybrid Decoupling: Governance and Systemic Risk Implications," in William W. Bratton & Joseph A. McCahery, eds., *Institutional Investor Activism* 351 (2015): "Some of these rights are economic, including dividend, liquidation, and appraisal rights under corporate law. Some rights are not purely monetary, including voting rights, director fiduciary duties, rights to bring suits and inspect corporate records, access to corporate proxy machinery. . . . Some of these rules are based on formal record ownership (even where the record owner passes voting rights to an economic owner); some are based on who holds voting rights. However, persons who have economic ownership but not voting rights are regulated lightly or, often, not at all."
4. See Anita Anand, *Governance Complexities in Firms with Dual Class Shares*, 3:3 Ann Corp Governance 184 (2018); Anita Anand, *The Success Stories of Dual-Class Shares Miss an Incontrovertible Truth*, Globe and Mail (2016), https://beta.theglobeandmail.com/report-on-business/rob-commentary/the-success-stories-of-dual-class-stocks-miss-an-incontrovertible-truth/article28830388; Anita Anand, *Offloading the Burden of Being Public: An Analysis of Multi-Voting Share Structures*, 10 Va L & Bus Rev (2016), https://papers.ssrn.com/sol3/papers.cfm?abstract_id=2728481.
5. In the United Kingdom, MVS structures have been strongly discouraged. Currently, the London Stock Exchange allows firms to list with multiple-voting classes only within the Standard Listing regime rather than the Premium Listing regime; United Kingdom, Financial Conduct Authority, *Listing Principles and Premium Listing Principles*, release 29, 7.2.1A, Premium Listing Principles 3 and 4. A 2017 discussion paper from the Financial Conduct Authority suggested the possibility of opening up the UK capital markets to multiple dual-class shares; Financial Conduct Authority, *Review of the Effectiveness of Primary Markets: The U.K. Primary Markets Landscape* 8 (2017), https://www.fca.org.uk/publication/discussion/dp17-02.pdf. This idea is controversial and has not been adopted at time of writing; Richard Burrows, *The UK Should Consider Dual-Class Listings Too*, MacFarlanes (2018), http://blog.macfarlanes.com/post/102eouh/the-uk-should-consider-dual-class-listings-too. For a historical study of MVSs in the United Kingdom, and in particular the role of investor culture and governance norms in limiting the popularity of MVS structures, see Fabio Braggion & Mariassunta Giannetti, *Changing Corporate Governance Norms: Evidence from Dual Class Shares in the U.K.*,

37 J Fin Intermediation 15 (2019). https://papers.ssrn.com/sol3/papers.cfm?abstract_id=.

6. There are currently at least eighty-six firms listed on the TSX with an MVS structure. The incidence of superior voting shares in TSX companies rose from 5 percent in 1975 to more than 15 percent in 1987. See Tara Gry, *Dual-Class Share Structures and Best Practicesin Corporate Governance* (Parliament of Canada, 2005), http://publications.gc.ca/collections/Collection-R/LoPBdP/PRB-e/PRB0526-e.pdf "An estimated 20 percent to 25 percent of companies listed on the TSX make use of some form of dual-class share structure or special voting rights. In comparison, in the United States, where rules on dual-class shares are much more restrictive and investor opposition is more vocal, just over 2 percent of companies issue restricted shares."
7. Drew Hasselback & Barbara Shecter, *From Cara Operations Ltd to Shopify Inc: Why Dual Class Shares Are Suddenly Cool Again*, Financial Post (2015), http://business.financialpost.com/news/fpstreet/from-cara-to-google-why-dual-class-shares-are-suddenly-cool-again.
8. Gry, *supra* note 6. Examples of this practice include some of Canada's most renowned and largest companies: Bombardier, Magna International, Rogers Communications, Shaw Communications, Alliance Atlantis Communications, Power Corp., Telus Corp., Quebecor, and Onex Corp., to name only a few. Both Magna and Telus are examples of previous MVS firms.
9. Tian Wen, *You Can't Sell Your Firm and Own It Too: Disallowing Dual-Class Stock Companies from Listing on Securities Exchanges*, 162 U Pa L Rev 1495 (2014).
10. Henrik Cronqvist & Mattias Nilsson, *Agency Costs of Controlling Minority Shareholders*, 38 J Fin QA 695 (2003); Harry DeAngelo & Linda DeAngelo, *Managerial Ownership of Voting Rights: A Study of Public Corporations with Dual Classes of Common Stock*, 14 J Fin Econ 33 (1985); Clas Bergstrom and Kristian Rydqvist, *Ownership of Equity in Dual-Class Firms*, 14 J Banking & Fin 255 (1990).
11. Andrew Hill, *Enrolment Open for an MBA in Murdoch*, Financial Times (2011), http://www.ft.com/cms/s/0/2fda9e8e-b176-11e0-9444-00144feab49a.html#axzz2IYIKmzDt, as cited by Wen, *supra* note 9.
12. Stephen M. Bainbridge, *What to Do about Dual Class Stock (If Anything)?* ProfessorBainbridge.com (2015), http://www.professorbainbridge.com/professorbainbridgecom/2015/11/what-to-do-about-dual-class-stock-if-anything.html.

13. Luigi Zingales, *The Value of a Voting Right: A Study of the Milan Stock Exchange Experience*, 7 Rev Fin Stud 125 (1994).
14. Ian Lee, *There Is a Logic in Dual-Class Shares*, National Post (2011), https://www.law.utoronto.ca/documents/lee/DualClassOpEd.pdf.
15. See Jensen & Meckling, *supra* preface note 3.
16. In the Canadian context, case law has made the preventive, forward-facing dimension of securities regulation explicit. In *Committee for the Equal Treatment of Asbestos Minority Shareholders v. Ontario (Securities Commission)*, [2001] 2 SCR 132 (Can), the Supreme Court of Canada confirmed that securities regulators have a legal duty to act in the public interest and to protect the public on a prospective and preventive basis. In the later case of *Cartaway Resources Corp. (Re)*, [2004] 1 SCR 672 (Can), at ¶ 61, the Supreme Court further held that regulators should use their public interest power to deter conduct that is deleterious to capital markets. This preventive approach is by no means unique to Canada. For the United Kingdom, see Financial Conduct Authority, *Our Approach to Enforcement* 2, 9 (2018), https://www.fca.org.uk/publication/corporate/our-approach-enforcement.pdf.
17. Ben Amoako-Adu et al., *Unification of Dual Class Shares in Canada with Clinical Case on Magna International* (Capital Markets Institute at the Rotman School of Management, 2011), https://www.rotman.utoronto.ca/-/media/Files/Programs-and-Areas/Institutes/CapitalMarkets/research/Unification%20Magna%20Research%20-Oct%2011.pdf.
18. See, for example, CBCA, *supra* chapter 1 note 25 at s 122. See also DGCL, *supra* chapter 3 note 92.
19. See *Foss v. Harbottle*, (1843) 67 Eng. Rep. 189 (V.C.) and related case law discussed in Jeffrey G. MacIntosh, *Minority Shareholder Rights in Canada and England*, 27 Osgoode Hall LJ 561 (1989).
20. They have, in all likelihood, paid a premium over market price of the publicly traded company in exchange for their control block. See Wayne Mikkelson & Hailu Regassa, *Premiums Paid in Block Transactions*, 12 Mgrl & Dec Econ 511 (1991).
21. CBCA, *supra* chapter 1 note 25 at s 137 and 143; Securities Exchange Act, 17 CFR § 240.14a-8 (1934); Companies Act, *supra* chapter 1 note 25 at c 46, s 292. I discuss shareholder proposals and the right to requisition meetings in Canada, the United States, and the United Kingdom in chapter 3. These rights are particularly important as means of achieving "proxy access" or nominating directors.

22. CBCA, *supra* chapter 1 note 25 at s 143; Companies Act, *supra* chapter 1 note 25 at s 303. American shareholders have no statutory right to requisition meetings.
23. This cause of action refers to an improper exercise of voting power by the majority of shareholders evidenced by the failure to cast votes for the benefit of the corporation as a whole. Such an action can allow minority shareholders to have a resolution voided after it has been passed upon a majority vote. For example, the court might void a resolution for alteration of the articles of association to allow the compulsory purchase of members' shares; *In re Tyco International Ltd.*, 340 F Supp 2d 94 (DNH 2004). Fraud on the minority permits a derivative suit when the plaintiff sufficiently pleads that a majority in control of a company perpetrated a fraud on the minority of the company: *Tomran Inc. v. Passano*, 862 A2d 453 (Md Ct Spec App 2004), *aff'd*, 891 A2d 336. See also *Fraud on the Minority Law & Legal Definition*, USLegal.com, http://definitions.uslegal.com/f/fraud-on-the-minority.
24. CBCA, *supra* chapter 1 note 25 at s 190; DGCL, *supra* chapter 3 note 92 at s 262.
25. CBCA, *supra* chapter 1 note 25 at s 241. In particular, where a shareholder believes that the affairs of a company have been conducted in an oppressive or unfairly prejudicial manner, he or she can apply to the court for a remedy.
26. The principle of majority rule has become somewhat diluted over time. See MacIntosh, *supra* note 19 at 562: "Majority rule has been transformed slowly over time, with increasing concern on the part of courts, legislators, and administrators for the protection of minority shareholders."
27. For example, see Wen, *supra* note 9.
28. Jeffrey G. MacIntosh et al., *The Puzzle of Shareholder Fiduciary Duties*, 19 CBLJ. 86 (1991).
29. Gry, *supra* note 6.
30. Borochin & Knopf, *supra* chapter 3 note 9. For further empirical analysis in support of this point, see also Anita Anand & Lorne Sossin, *Independence and Accountability in Public and Private Governance*, 61:1 Can Pub Admin (2018), https://doi.org/10.1111/capa.12268.
31. CBCA, *supra* chapter 1 note 25 at s 241.
32. Andrew Winden, *Sunrise, Sunset: An Empirical and Theoretical Assessment of Dual-Class Stock Structures*, 2018:3 Colum Bus L Rev 852 (2018), https://papers.ssrn.com/sol3/papers.cfm?abstract_id=3001574.
33. Daines & Klausner, *supra* chapter 2 note 60.

34. Anand (2018), *supra* note 4; Lucian A. Bebchuk & Kobi Kastiel, *The Untenable Case for Perpetual Dual-Class Stock*, 103 Va L Rev 585 (2017), https://papers.ssrn.com/sol3/papers.cfm?abstract_id=2954630.
35. Thomas J. Chemmanur & Yawen Jian, *Dual Class IPOs: A Theoretical Analysis*, 36 Corp J Banking & Fin 306 (2012), www.sciencedirect.com/science/article/pii/S0378426611002214. Richard Squire has mentioned in response to this argument that founders may also make the mistake of selecting a single-class structure when they should have selected an MVS structure. But this argument is unpersuasive in my view, given that a single-class structure does not bear the normative failings of MVSs and in particular the decoupling of equity from control in a systematic way. See Anand (2018), *supra* note 4.
36. Fairfax Financial Holdings, *Fairfax Calls Special Shareholders' Meeting to Consider Amendment to Terms of Multiple Voting Shares*, Fairfax News (2015), http://www.Fairfax.ca/news/press-releases/press-release-details/2015/Fairfax-Calls-Special-Shareholders-Meeting-to-Consider-Amendment-to-Terms-of-Multiple-Voting-Shares/default.aspx.
37. Richard Squire, email correspondence on file with author, December 27, 2017.
38. *Magna International Inc. (Re)* (2010), 34 OSC Bull 1290 (OSC). I have presented a developed argument along these lines in Anita Anand, "Was Magna in the Public Interest?" 49 Osgoode Hall LJ 311 at 312 (2012).
39. *Magna, id.* at ¶ 103.
40. *Id.*
41. See Ben Amaoko-Adu et al., *Magna: The True Cost of Share Unification*, Can Investment Rev (2011), http://www.investmentreview.com/analysis-research/magna-the-true-cost-of-share-unification-5694. The authors compare Stronach's percentage return what other companies paid their controlling shareholders who held superior voting shares. Of the thirty-one previous cases of unification on the TSX, only one had a special payout to the controlling shareholder similar in magnitude to the payout to Magna's founder.
42. See also remarks by Justice Wilton-Siegel following the Magna transaction, in Tim Kiladze, *Magna Board "Spectacularly" Vacated Field: Judge*, Globe and Mail (2011), https://www.theglobeandmail.com/report-on-business/streetwise/magna-board-spectacularly-vacated-field-judge/article611970/.
43. Iacobucci, *supra* chapter 2 note 53.

44. Steve Sauerwald et al., *Expressive Shareholder Democracy: A Multilevel Study of Shareholder Dissent in 15 Western European CountriesI,* 53 J Mgmt Stud 520 (2015), onlinelibrary.wiley.com/doi/10.1111/joms.12171/full.
45. Peter Iliev et al., *Shareholder Voting and Corporate Governance around the World*, 28 Rev Fin Stud 2167 (2015), https://academic.oup.com/rfs/article/28/8/2167/1599500/Shareholder-Voting-and-Corporate-Governance-Around.
46. *Id.* at 2168.
47. Such a disclosure requirement may have been useful at the recent Bombardier annual general meeting, where the management was happy to report that more than 90 percent of shareholders voted to reelect the board of directors and also voted in favor of a hotly contested executive compensation package. See Ross Marowitz, *Ontario Teachers' Pension Plan Votes Against Bombardier Chair*, Toronto Star (2017), https://www.thestar.com/business/2017/05/09/ontario-teachers-pension-plan-votes-against-bombardier-chair.html. Regarding comply-or-explain generally, see Anand, *supra* chapter 2 note 57;Anita Anand et al., *Domestic and International Influences on Firm-Level Governance: Evidence from Canada*, 14 Am L & Econ Rev 68 (2011).
48. Ontario Securities Commission, *MI 61-101 Protection of Minority Security Holders in Special Transactions and Companion Policy 61-101CP Protection of Minority Security Holders in Special Transactions* (2008), https://www.osc.gov.on.ca/documents/en/Securities-Category6/rule_20080201_61-101_protect-minority.pdf. See also Ontario Securities Commission, *Rule 56-601 Restricted Shares* (2015), which compels issuers of MVSs to make specific disclosure regarding characteristics of shares in offering documents.
49. Ontario Securities Commission, *Multilateral Instrument 61-101 Protection of Minority Security Holders in Special Transactions* (2017).
50. *Id.* at s 2.3.
51. The law regarding valuations has been controversial in terms of information that is disclosed to shareholders. See *Re InterOil Corp.*, 2017 YKSC 16.
52. Robert J. Jackson Jr., *Perpetual Dual-Class Stock: The Case against Corporate Royalty*, address delivered at UC Berkeley School of Law, 2018), https://www.sec.gov/news/speech/perpetual-dual-class-stock-case-against-corporate-royalty#_ftn19.
53. Canadian Securities Administrators, *Multilateral CSA Staff Notice 61-302 Staff Review and Commentary on Multilateral Instrument 61-101 Protection of Minority Security Holders in Special Transactions* (2017),

https://www.osc.gov.on.ca/documents/en/Securities-Category6/csa_20170727_61-302_sn-staff-review.pdf. Securities regulators in Alberta, Manitoba, and New Brunswick adopted MI 61-101 in 2017; *Securities Commission Staff Raise the Bar for Conflict Transactions* (Osler, 2017), https://www.osler.com/en/resources/regulations/2017/le-personnel-de-la-commission-des-valeurs-mobilier.

54. Mindy B. Gilbert et al., *Boards Beware: Regulators Actively Monitoring Related Party Transactions*, (Davies LLP, 2017), https://www.dwpv.com/en/Insights/Publications/2017/Boards-Beware-Regulators-Actively-Monitoring-Related-Party-Transactions.

Chapter 6

1. Jeffrey G. MacIntosh, *The Poison Pill: A Noxious Nostrum for Canadian Shareholders* 15 CBLJ 276 (1989).
2. This is known as a "flip-in" provision (the most common type), which typically states that upon the acquisition of a certain percentage (10 or 20 percent) of the target's outstanding securities, each right other than those held by the bidder entitles its holder upon payment to acquire the target's securities having a market value equal to some multiple (e.g., two times) of the exercise price. See Macabacus.com, *Poison Pill*, https://www.macabacus.com/defense/poison-pill.
3. Marcel Kahan & Edward B. Rock, *How I Learned to Stop Worrying and Love the Pill*, 69 U Chicago L Rev 871 (2002).
4. See *Re Royal Host Real Estate Investment Trust* (1999), 8 ASCS 3672, http://www.asc.ca/Notices%20Decisions%20Orders%20%20Rulings/Issuers/6974_Royal_Host_Real_Estate_Investment_Trust_(The)_-_Reasons_-_1999-11-24.pdf.
5. Certain cases have evidenced an alternative regulatory approach, but they are the exception rather than the norm. See, e.g., *Re Neo Materials Technologies Inc.*, 2009 LNONOSC 638, https://www.osc.gov.on.ca/documents/en/Proceedings-RAD/rad_20090901_neo-material.pdf; *Re Pulse Data Inc.*, 2007 ABASC 895, http://albertasecurities.com/Notices%20Decisions%20Orders%20%20Rulings/Issuers/Pulse%20Data%20Inc_Nov30.pdf.
6. Kahan & Rock, *supra* chapter 1 note 9.
7. David Kershaw, *The Illusion of Importance: Reconsidering the U.K.'s Takeover Defence Prohibition* 56:2 Intl & Comp LQ 267, 272 (2007); *A Guide to Takeovers in the United Kingdom* (SlaughterandMay.com, 2010),

http://www.slaughterandmay.com/media/39320/a_guide_to_takeovers_in_the_uk_mar_2010.pdf. See also UK Panel on Takeovers and Mergers, City Code on Takeovers and Mergers, General Principle 3 and Rule 21 (12th ed., 2018).

8. Canadian Securities Administrators (CSA), Ontario Securities Commission, *Proposed Amendments to Multilateral Instrument 62-104 Take-Over Bids and Issuer Bids, Proposed Changes to National Policy 62-203 Take-Over Bids and Issuer Bids, and Proposed Consequential Amendments* (2015), http://www.osc.gov.on.ca/documents/en/Securities-Category6/csa_20150331_62-104_rfc-proposed-admendments-multilateral-instrument.pdf. At one point in the process, the Autorité des Marchés Financiers and the Ontario Securities Commission were divided in their approaches to the issues. For the early AMF position, see Autorité des Marchés Financiers, *An Alternative Approach to Securities Regulators' Intervention in Defensive Tactics* (2013), https://lautorite.qc.ca/fileadmin/lautorite/consultations/fin-2013-06/2013mars14-avis-amf-62-105-cons-publ-en.pdf. See also Canadian Securities Administrators (CSA), *CSA Notice 62-306: Update on Proposed National Instrument 62-105 Security Holder Rights Plans*, and Autorité des Marchés Financiers, *An Alternative Approach to Securities Regulators' Intervention in Defensive Tactics* (2014), http://www.osc.gov.on.ca/en/SecuritiesLaw_rule_20140911_62-306_update-holder-rights-plan.htm, which sets out some of the history.
9. Canadian Securities Administrators (CSA), *CSA Notice of Amendments to Take-Over Bid Regime* (2016), http://www.osc.gov.on.ca/en/SecuritiesLaw_csa_20160225_62-104_amd-take-over-bids.htm.
10. In terms of actual legislation, Canada's takeover-bid regime was introduced following the significant recommendations contained in the *Kimber Report*. An important review of takeover-bid legislation occurred in 1983 with the "Report of the Three Wise Men." See Ontario Securities Commission, *Report of the Committee to Review the Provisions of the Securities Act (Ontario) Relating to Take-Over Bids and Issuer Bids* (1983). Further reforms to the regime occurred in 1987 after the introduction of National Policy 38 "Take-Over Bids—Defensive Tactics." Prior to the CSA proposal, the most recent review of takeover-bid law in Canada occurred in 1996 with the introduction of the Zimmerman amendments, which, among other things, lengthened the bid period from twenty-one to thirty-five days. See *Report of the Committee to Review Take-Over Bid Time Limits* (1996). For history, see Mary Condon et al., *Securities Law in Canada: Cases and Commentary* (2nd ed., 2010).

11. CSA, *supra* note 9 at 2.
12. CBCA, *supra* chapter 1 note 25 at s 122(1)(a)(b).
13. *Stone v. Ritter*, 911 A2d 362 (Del 2006). See also Strine et al., *supra* chapter 2 note 11.; and DGCL, *supra* chapter 3 note 92 at ss. 102(b)(7), 141, 144, and 145.
14. See, for example, the US case of *Moran v. Household International Inc.*, 500 A2d 1346 (Del 1985), and *Unocal Corp. v. Mesa Petroleum Co.*, 493 A2d 946 (Del 1985). See *Pente Investment Management Ltd. v. Schneider Corp.*, 1998 14808 (ONSC). The court in *Pente* held that directors must seek the best value reasonably available to shareholders, but there is no duty to auction. The court in the case reasoned that an auction is often the best way to achieve the best value but not the exclusive way. In the case at bar, the board of directors acted in good faith and with reasonable investigation and therefore received benefit of the business-judgment rule (BJR).
15. See *Peoples, supra* chapter 1 note 20.
16. See *BCE Inc. v. 1976 Debentureholders*, 2008 SCC 69 [2008] 3 SCR 560. The American BJR is more deferential to boards; Sharfman, *supra* chaspter 3 note 24.
17. *Id.* at ¶ 112.
18. *Id.* at ¶ 66: "the directors owe a fiduciary duty to the corporation, and only to the corporation . . . directors owe their duty to the corporation, not to stakeholders."
19. See *Revlon Inc. v. MacAndrews & Forbes Holdings Inc.*, 506 A2d 173 (Del 1986).
20. *BCE, supra* note 16 at ¶ 42.
21. See *id.* at ¶ 66. The Court builds on the decision in *Peoples, supra* chapter 1 note 20. The SCC in *Peoples* held that the board *may* consider the impact of corporate decisions on shareholders "or particular groups of stakeholders," which include "the interests of shareholders, employees, suppliers, creditors, consumers, governments and the environment," at ¶ 39. For a thoughtful analysis of the treatment of employees in hostile bids, see Anthony Niblett, *Hostile Takeovers and Overreliance*, 38 Seattle U L Rev 595 (2015).
22. Patrick Lupa, *The BCE Blunder: An Argument in Favour of Shareholder Wealth Maximization in the Change of Control Context*, 20 Dal J Legal Stud 1 (2011).
23. Edward Iacobucci, *Indeterminacy and the Canadian Court's Approach to Corporate Fiduciary Duties*, 48 Can J Bus L 232, 242 (2009). See also Jeffrey G. MacIntosh, *BCE and the Peoples' Corporate Law: Learning to Live on*

Quicksand, 48:2 CBLJ 255 (2009). MacIntosh states that with respect to *BCE* and *Peoples*, "Although much of both decisions is per incuriam, obiter dictum, or both, these rulings have thrown the most basic principles of corporate law into a state of uncertainty and confusion" (at 1).

24. According to Delaware jurisprudence, "fiduciary duties are owed by the director and officers to the corporation and its stockholders"; *Arnold v. Soc'y for Sav Bancorp Inc.*, 678 A2d 533 (Del 1996) at 539. While the obligation to maximize shareholder value under Delaware law clarifies the meaning of this duty to "the corporation and its stockholders" in changes of control, the reference here to the "corporation" as a beneficiary of the duty raises the same normative ambiguity as we see in *BCE*.
25. MacIntosh, *supra* note 23. See also Anita Anand, "Duties of Directors after the Financial Crisis," in Adolfo Paolini, ed., *Research Handbook on Directors' Duties* 321–338 (2014).
26. *Shlensky v. Wrigley*, 95 Ill App. 2d 173, 237 NE 2d 776 (1968); *Otis & Co. v. Pennsylvania R. Co.*, 61 F Supp 905 (DC Pa 1945). For discussion of the onus-shifting device inherent in the US context, see Doug Harris et al., *Cases, Materials and Notes on Partnerships and Canadian Business Corporations* 342 (4th ed., 2004). Note also that in the context of a hostile takeover bid, courts will apply more stringent scrutiny. In the context of a hostile takeover, courts will apply the more stringent test in *Unocal v. Mesa Petroleum Co.* 493 A2d 946 (Del 1985). It is also referred to as intermediate scrutiny. Prior to *Unocal*, the Delaware courts had applied the BJR to takeover defenses, mergers, and sales. In *Unocal*, it was held that a board of directors may only try to prevent a takeover if it can be shown that there is a threat to corporate policy and the course of action taken to prevent the takeover is proportional and reasonable given the nature of the threat. The decision in *Unocal* was in many ways a response to the reaction following *Paramount*, which was criticized because it allowed the directors to focus on the longer term, rather than the shorter term, in deciding what to do. Subsequent Delaware cases such as *Unocal* have greatly confined the ability of directors to focus on the long term, encouraging them to focus on what is best for shareholders in the short term. See also *Revlon, supra* note 20.
27. See *id.* at Schedule A, *Approaches to Defensive Tactics in the United States and United Kingdom.* For the United Kingdom, see the City Code on Takeovers and Mergers, http://www.thetakeoverpanel.org.uk/the-code/download-code. The code places many more restrictions on the target board than would apply in Canada. The code "prohibits a target company

board from taking any action during a bid, or in anticipation of a bid, that would frustrate the take-over bid or otherwise deny shareholders the opportunity to decide on its merits, unless such action is approved by target company shareholders in the face of the bid."

28. See *Unocal Corp. v Mesa Petroleum*, 493 A2d 946 (Del 1985).
29. *Paramount Communications Inc. v. QVC Network Inc.*, 637 A2d 34 (Del 1994), Civil Action No 5249-CC (Del) (Ch 2011) (QL).
30. *Revlon Inc. v. MacAndrews & Forbes Holdings Inc.*, 506 A2d 173 (Del 1986).
31. See Kahan & Rock, *supra* chapter 2 note 9.
32. See Kevin J. Thomson et al., *When "No" Means "Maybe"—The State of the "Just Say No" Defense in Canada* (Davies Ward Phillips & Vineberg LLP, 2011), https://www.dwpv.com/~/media/Files/PDF_EN/2014-2007/Davies_Ward_-_When_No_Means_Maybe.ashx .
33. The jurisprudence on this point emerges from securities commission cases, as discussed in the next section. This is a point to which the AMF responded in its report, *supra* note 8.
34. Anand, *supra* note 25 at 321–338.
35. Securities Act, *supra* chapter 2 note 64 at s 1.1. For the United States, see also Securities and Exchange Commission, supra chapter 2 note 62. For the United Kingdom, see Financial Conduct Authority, *supra* chapter 2 note 63.
36. See Rob Yalden, *Canadian Mergers and Acquisitions at the Crossroads*, 55 CBLJ 389 (2014), who agrees that the objectives of corporate law and securities regulation are at odds.
37. MacIntosh, *supra* note 1. Under Canadian securities law, takeover-bid rules trigger once the bidder crosses the 20 percent shareholding threshold; Multilateral Instrument 62-104 at s 1.1. In the United States, there is no such bright-line rule, and the triggers for tender-offer rules are more qualitative; see *Wellman v. Dickinson*, 475 F Supp 783 (SDNY 1979).
38. Macabacus.com, *supra* note 2.
39. MacIntosh, *supra* note 1.
40. *Id.* at 278–279. See also Jeffrey MacIntosh, *Poison Pills in Canada: A Reply to Dey and Yalden*, 17 CBLJ 323, 334 (1991). Some may question what the proper role of the board is if shareholder have the sole say in whether to tender to the bid. Boards should evaluate the bid(s) and make a recommendation to shareholders.
41. Securities Act, *supra* chapter 2 note 64 at ss 97(1) and 97.2(1). For the American equivalent, see the "all-holders" and "best-price" rules; Securities Exchange Act, *supra* chapter 3 note 75 Rule 14d–10. See Anita

Anand, *Regulating Issuer Bids: The Case of the Dutch Auction*, 45 McGill LJ 133 (2000), for a review of the principle of equal treatment in securities regulation. On the point of the discriminatory effects of poison pills, see MacIntosh, *supra* note 40, written in reply to Peter Dey and Robert Yalden, *Keeping the Playing Field Level: Poison Pills and Directors' Fiduciary Duties in Canadian Take-Over Law*, 17 CBLJ 252 (1991); and Yalden, *supra* note 36. Note, however, that it appears that no court or securities commission has struck down a poison pill on the basis that it discriminated among shareholders qua shareholders.

42. Michael S. Weisbach, *Outside Directors and CEO Turnover*, 20 J Fin Econ 416, 435 (1988).
43. As Jensen and Meckling explain, if both parties to an agency relationship "are utility maximizers, there is good reason to believe that the agent will not always act in the best interests of the principal"; Jensen & Meckling, *supra* preface note 3 at 309.
44. *Kimber Report, supra* chapter 1 note 14; *347883 Alberta Ltd. v. Producers Pipelines Ltd.* (1991), 80 DLR (4th) 359 (Sask CA).
45. See *Producers Pipelines, id.*; see also MacIntosh, *supra* note 1. In the era of high executive compensation, the management entrenchment hypothesis continues to have force and relevance. Allaire seems to suggest that the management entrenchment hypothesis has less, not more, relevance in today's world: "the quaint notion that management is, ipso facto, against the takeover of its company because of inherent conflicts of interest must be updated." See Yvan Allaire, "Counterpoint: Canada Needs a New Regime for Hostile Takeovers," Financial Post (2014), http://business.financialpost.com/2014/04/30/counterpoint-canada-needs-a-new-regime-for-hostile-takeovers/>. Yet Allaire does not explain the ways, if any, in which this may be true. As long as agents run a corporation (i.e., a legal fiction), one will need to be concerned with agents seeking to entrench themselves.
46. Andrei Shleifer & Robert W. Vishny, *Management Entrenchment: The Case of Manager-Specific Investments*, 25 J Fin Econ 123 (1989). While the existence of golden parachutes may make members of senior management less reluctant to abdicate their positions, there is as of yet no empirical study indicating that this is indeed the case.
47. *Kimber Report, supra* chapter 1 note 14; *Producers Pipelines, supra* note 45.
48. The Williams Act, America's first federal tender-offer legislation, was initially motivated by concerns that corporate raiders were taking over "proud old companies." It was later reformed in response to a number of

concerns, including managerial entrenchment. Richard A. Booth, *The Problem with Federal Tender Offer Law*, 77:4 Cal L Rev 707, 711 (1989); Thomas Hurst, *The Regulation of Tender Offers in the United States and the United Kingdom: Self-Regulation versus Legal Regulation*, 12:3 NCJ Intl L & Com Reg 389, 405 (1987).

49. *Neo Materials Technologies Inc., supra* note 5 at 91, 103.
50. MacIntosh, *supra* note 1.
51. See Yalden, *supra* note 36.
52. Bernard S. Black, *Shareholder Passivity Reexamined*, 89 Mich L Rev 520 (1990).
53. See CSA, *supra* note 8.
54. Recent TSX amendments mean that for TSX-listed issuers, which, of course, do not include companies listed on the TSX Venture Exchange, each director other than a listed issuer that is majority controlled must be elected by a majority of votes cast.
55. Note, for example, the proxy processes of Hess, Allergan, and Agrium. See Christopher Helman, *Elliott and Hess Trade Tit for Tat ahead of Proxy Showdown*, Forbes (2010), http://www.forbes.com/sites/christopherhelman/2013/05/13/two-sides-spar-ahead-of-hess-corp-annual-meeting/>; Liz Hoffman, *Proxy Firm ISS Urges Shareholder Vote at Allergan*, Wall Street Journal (2014), http://www.wsj.com/articles/proxy-firm-iss-urges-shareholder-vote-at-allergan-1412175544.
56. See Stephanie Ben-Ishai & Poonam Puri, *The Canadian Oppression Remedy Judicially Considered: 1995–2001*, 30 Queen's LJ 79 (2004).
57. If it is the case that management seeks to entrench itself, then it stands to reason that there would be fewer takeover bids in jurisdictions in which boards are entitled to just say no. Specifically, if takeovers were significantly easier to complete in Canada, the proportion of successful bids per corporation should be significantly higher in Canada than in the United States. To test this hypothesis, we compared the proportions of successful takeover bids in Canada and the United States to the number of registered corporations in each country (our data included corporations that had at least $1 billion in market capitalization and were involved in a takeover bid registered in the Capital IQ database over the past ten years). We found that Canada experienced 17.8 percent more successful takeover bids per corporation than the United States, although Canada and the United States had no significant difference in the proportion of successful bids relative to total bids (at a 0.1 confidence level). This suggests that Canada has more total takeover bids but that the bids are not any more likely to

be successful than in the United States. To account for the difference in baseline takeover-bid activity in the two countries, we examined industry composition as a possible source of the difference. When comparing similar industries across the border, we did not find any significant difference in either total bids or the proportion of successful bids. We did find that the energy market is more active and is relatively larger in Canada, though, which would account for the difference in total number of takeover bids between the two countries while substantiating the similar takeover-bid success rates. The data also indicated that Canada has more successful hostile takeover bids per registered corporation than the United States but the same proportion of successful hostile takeovers per hostile bid. Although the success rates per hostile bid are the same, the fact that there are more total successful hostile bids in Canada relative to the number of corporations would give some credence to the notion that Canada is more bidder-friendly. The data, however, are still inconclusive; the absence of clear evidence suggesting that Canadian rules are too bidder-friendly may still support the countering argument, namely, that the argument against our current securities regime is overstated. See Anita Anand, *The Future of Poison Pills in Canada: Are Takeover Bid Reforms Needed?*, 61:1 McGill LJ 1 (2015).

58. See *CTC Dealer Holdings Ltd./Canadian Tire Corp. Ltd.* (1987) 10 OSC Bull. 509 (Can On).
59. For key examples of the differing approaches to adjudicating poison pills, see *Neo Materials Technologies Inc., supra* note 5; *Pulse Data Inc., supra* note 5; *Abitibi Bowater Inc. (Produits forestiers Résolu) v. Fibrek Inc.*, 2012 QCCA 569, EYB 2012-204457, 100 BLR (4th) 265 (Que CA), leave to appeal to SCC refused 435 NR 389 (note); *Hudbay Minerals Inc. and Augusta Resource Corp.*, (Re) 2014 BCSECCOM 153. As Adrian Myers states, "regulators, not shareholders, are the ones who determine whether a hostile takeover succeeds or fails. By forcing companies to abandon takeover defences after arbitrary periods of time, regulators leave shareholders vulnerable not just to hostile bidders but to unexpected turns of fate." See Adrian Myers, *Regulators Should Get Out of Takeovers*, Globe and Mail (2014). See also Anita Anand, *Carving the Public Interest in Securities Regulation*, 57:2 UTLJ 293 (2007).
60. CSA, *supra* note 9.
61. See Janet McFarland, *Regulators Unveil New Rules for Takeover Bids*, Globe and Mail (2018), http://www.theglobeandmail.com/report-on-business/regulators-unveil-new-rules-for-takeover-bids/article23708641.

62. See James C. Tory et al., *Canadian Securities Regulators' Decisions on Poison Pills Diverge* (Torys LLP, 2010), https://www.torys.com/Publications/Documents/Publication%20PDFs/MA2010-4.pdf.
63. See Jeffrey MacIntosh, *The Role of Institutional and Retail Investors in Canadian Capital Markets*, 31:2 Osgoode Hall LJ 372 (1993).
64. See current law contained in Part XX of the OSA at ss 95(1) and 95(2). See *supra* text accompanying note.
65. These are the "Revlon duties" pursuant to which directors in a sale of control become "defenders of the corporate bastion to auctioneers charged with getting the best price for the stockholders at a sale of the company." See Robert Monks and Neil Minow, *Corporate Governance* (2008).
66. See Anita Anand, *New Canadian Securities Administrators' Rules Would Discourage Takeover Bids*, National Post (2015).
67. Douglas Bryce et al., *New Take-Over Bid Regime* (2016), https://www.osler.com/en/resources/critical-situations/2016/new-take-over-bid-regime.
68. CSA, *supra* note 8 at s 2(3).
69. As MacIntosh states, *supra* note 41 at 332, "The mandatory minimum offer period allows other prospective acquirors time to formulate a competing offer, driving up the acquisition price and reducing the gains to the initial bidder. It also allowed self-interested management . . . time to formulate a defensive response that will either defeat a hostile bid or generate a much higher acquisition price."
70. See *supra* text accompanying notes 13 and 14.
71. CSA, *supra* note 8 at s 2.28.
72. Of course, the reforms did not go all the way to ensuring that shareholders' interests will be protected in takeovers. It may be the case that instead of relying on poison pills, target boards will implement other defensive tactics (asset sales or private placements, for example) as they have a lengthy period of 105 days in which to do so. It seems plausible that regulatory intervention may occur as a result of tactics other than poison pills. Furthermore, nothing seems to prohibit target boards from implementing tactical pills prior to the expiration of the 105-day bid period. With no national securities regulator in place in Canada, it is possible that individual jurisdictions will address tactical pills differently and the fragmentation that has plagued the takeover-bid regime in the past will continue.

Chapter 7

1. Amir N. Licht, *Social Norms and the Law: Why Peoples Obey the Law*, 4:3 Rev L Econ 715 (2008).
2. *Id.*
3. Dionysia Katelouzou, *Myths and Realities of Hedge Fund Activism: Some Empirical Evidence*, 7 Va L & Bus Rev 459 (2013); Andrew Carrothers, *Friends or Foes? Activist Hedge Funds and Other Institutional Investors* 3:17 Eco & Bus Rev 38 (2017).

Index

For the benefit of digital users, indexed terms that span two pages (e.g., 52–53) may, on occasion, appear on only one of those pages.

Tables and figures are indicated by *t* and *f* following the page number